Intelligence in Animals

INTELLIGENCE IN ANIMALS

PUBLISHED BY

THE READER'S DIGEST ASSOCIATION LIMITED

LONDON NEW YORK MONTREAL SYDNEY CAPE TOWN

INTELLIGENCE IN ANIMALS
Produced by Toucan Books Limited, London for
The Reader's Digest Association Limited, London
with Bradbury and Williams

Written by Michael Bright
First English Copyright © 1994
The Reader's Digest Association, Limited

The photo credits that appear on page 160
are hereby made a part of this copyright page.

Library of Congress Cataloging in Publication Data
Intelligence in animals.
        p.   cm – (The earth, its wonders, its secrets)
    Includes index.
    ISBN 0-89577-913-7
    1. Animal intelligence. 2. Animal behavior. I. Reader's
Digest Association. II. Series.
QL785.I58 1997
591.5'13 – dc21

Printed in the United States of America

CONTENTS

THE SECRETS OF INTELLIGENCE

Scientists and philosophers from the time of Aristotle to the mid-19th century believed that the lives of animals were guided by instinct alone. Then the Englishman Charles Darwin made the daring assertion that animals can reason.

Are animals intelligent? Scientists who study them and the way in which they behave cannot agree on an answer. Some would say that a horse is intelligent because it can respond to simple commands from its rider; others argue that if a horse was really intelligent, it would not consent to be ridden. And if the large-brained dolphin is as intelligent as some believe, why does it allow itself to be caught in nets and then locked up in an aquarium? Should a domestic dog be called intelligent because it gains a free meal and a comfortable home from humans?

Before the English naturalist Charles Darwin wrote and published *The Descent of Man* in 1871, scientists believed that an animal's entire life was controlled by instinct – that is, a series of innate instructions handed down from generation to generation. Animals, they believed, showed no signs of true intelligence (an ability to reason); indeed, it was the possession of this quality that separated man from beast. Darwin challenged this view. He proposed that 'animals possess some power of reasoning' and that 'the differences in mind between man and the higher animals, great as it is, certainly is one of degree and not kind'.

Darwin based his views on observations gained during his world travels. Whilst visiting South America, for instance, his attention had been drawn to the behaviour of a troupe of New World monkeys. The monkeys were given soft-boiled eggs. At first they smashed them, spilling much of the contents in the process. But gradually they learned to hit one end gently against something hard and pick off the bits of shell with their fingers. They were also offered lumps of sugar wrapped in paper, some of which contained live wasps. In their haste to get at the sugar, the monkeys were stung. However, having experienced a painful sting just once, the monkeys quickly learned to be more cautious. Before opening the paper, they would hold the packet to the ear to detect any movement inside.

It was a rather cruel experiment, thought Darwin, but it supported his theories. Further evidence came to his attention from sources closer to home in England, such as a resourceful gun dog belonging to a sportsman called Colonel Hutchinson.

During a shooting drive two partridges were shot simultaneously, one killed, the other wounded. The injured bird fluttered away and was caught by the retriever, but returning to her master the dog came across the dead bird. 'She stopped,' recalled the colonel, 'evidently greatly puzzled, and after one or two trials, finding she could not take it up without permitting escape of the winged bird, she considered a moment, then deliberately murdered it, by giving it a severe crunch, and afterwards brought away both together. This was the only known instance of her having wilfully injured any game.'

The action of the dog in killing the bird was decisive, Darwin reckoned, for it ran quite contrary to the instincts of the breed and its training. It was further evidence that animals can call upon higher mental faculties. At the time, the suggestion was tantamount to heresy.

Nevertheless, Darwin's views opened the floodgates. By the turn of the century, all kinds of bizarre ways in which animals behaved were offered as evidence of their intelligence. Some became legends in their own time. Greyfriars Bobby was one.

BELOVED BOBBY

The year after Darwin published his great work, a dog was buried with considerable pomp and ceremony in the Greyfriars district of Edinburgh. The dog, called Bobby, was a Skye terrier and he belonged to Auld Jock (John Gray), an impoverished shepherd from the Pentland Hills. Jock had died in 1858 and had been buried in an Edinburgh churchyard. The event was witnessed by the vicar, by a gravedigger and, despite a 'No Dogs Allowed' notice, by Bobby. The churchyard workers tried to chase the dog away, but he returned every day to his master's grave. A fallen tombstone served him as a kennel, and meals, usually a bowl of broth, were provided each day by the Greyfriars Dining Room, an eating house frequented by Auld Jock.

A few years after his master's death, Bobby was arrested by the police as an unlicensed vagrant, and was about to be put down when the Lord Provost paid for the dog's licence. Bobby died of natural causes several years later and was buried next to Auld Jock.

What had spurred the dog to behave in such a way? Was he an intelligent, sensitive creature, conscious of his master's demise and present position in the grave? Or was he merely following the habits of a lifetime, commuting more or less automatically between a familiar resting place and an equally familiar source of food at the eating house Auld Jock had visited regularly when alive? We will never know the answer, though tales have certainly abounded since Darwin's time of 'super-intelligent' dogs and other animals.

One of the most famous was Rolf, a terrier living with the Moekel family in Mannheim, Germany. His story emerged in 1913 when scientists revealed that this dog could do sums, not just simple counting, but calculations as complicated as cube roots. Rolf's owners had discovered his mathematical prowess when Paula, their young daughter, was struggling with some basic arithmetic homework. In desperation the girl's mother looked at Rolf, asking whether he could give her the sum of two plus two. Frau Moekel was more than surprised when Rolf trotted over and tapped his paw on her arm four times. Another child asked him to add five and five, and without hesitation, so the story goes, the dog tapped out ten. In a short time the family found that he could work out simple additions, subtractions and multiplications, and there was even more to come.

Rolf created his own alphabet, the family reading out the letters A to Z and Rolf tapping out the number he had assigned to each letter. Incredibly, like the scoring system in

DARWIN RIDICULED *People were not flattered to be told that they were related to apes.*

FAITHFUL FRIEND *The Skye terrier 'Greyfriars Bobby' showed great devotion to his late master.*

the game Scrabble, the dog gave the lowest numbers to the most commonly used letters. Numbers also represented key instructions, such as 'yes', 'no', 'I'm hungry', 'go out' and 'time for bed'. Many sceptical mathematicians and psychologists descended on the Moekel household to test the dog, but Rolf proved that he could sort and count objects of different colours and identify pictures of familiar animals.

Rolf died in 1919, but one of his offspring, Lola, carried on the family tradition, becoming even more of a celebrity. Lola could tap out units with her right paw and tens with her left. Even more remarkably, she could answer sums that were written down. The scientists of the time were stumped for an explanation.

THE TALE OF CLEVER HANS

A clue came from another part of Germany, Berlin, and the story of Clever Hans. Clever Hans was a horse, an Arab stallion from Russia. In 1900 he was bought by Wilhelm von Osten, a retired schoolmaster. Osten was convinced that animals

SUPER-HORSE *Clever Hans astonished the world's academics. He seemed to be able to count and work out simple calculations.*

possess an intelligence equal to that of man, and had spent much of his spare time trying to prove the point. He had started by trying to teach a rather troublesome bear and a dimwitted cart-horse how to do simple arithmetic. Neither animal, however, showed the slightest inclination to fill their heads with multiplication, division, addition or subtraction. But Clever Hans seemed to be of a different calibre altogether.

Osten taught the horse the numbers one to nine first with the help of a row of skittles. He then replaced the skittles with numbers on a blackboard. A sum was drawn up on the blackboard and Clever Hans tapped his hoof on the ground to give the answer. In a short time, Clever Hans could work out reasonably complex

calculations, including square roots. Scientific observers were astonished, and, try as they might, they could see no signs of trickery. After some tests by an eminent mathematician, the horse was considered to have the mathematical capability of a 14-year-old schoolchild.

Clever Hans and his owner enjoyed worldwide acclaim, but the scientific community was sceptical and a group of leading professors was asked to subject the horse to five weeks of intense scrutiny. On every test Clever Hans got his sums right. Then one of the scientists, Oskar Pfungst, a psychologist from Berlin, had an inspiration. Could Hans get the correct answers if the horse alone could see the numbers? While one of the team wrote down the numbers and left the room, everyone else, including Osten, moved behind the blackboard. Of all those remaining in the room, only the horse knew which calculation was set on the blackboard. Clever Hans failed every subsequent test.

What the horse had been doing, proposed Pfungst, was to take 'cues', either from its trainer or from the other people in the room. It was able to spot very subtle movements, such as a minute nod of the head, and to detect the tension experienced by everyone in the room as it reached the correct answer. Scientists have since discovered that horses (and dogs) can pick up the heartbeat of someone standing nearby: as Clever Hans drew close to the answer, an increase in everyone's heartbeat indicated the place for it to stop tapping. Osten had not deliberately set out to deceive, but had influenced the experiment unintentionally. The Clever Hans story illustrates the difficulty in testing animals for evidence of intelligence.

At about the same time that Clever Hans and the dogs Rolf and Lola were performing their tricks, another famous animal was impressing psychologists with his 400-word vocabulary. He was Fellow, a German shepherd dog, who also starred in

NEW TRICKS *The American Edward Lee Thorndike tried to measure animals' abilities to learn from experience.*

several movies, including *Chief of the Pack*. Fellow's owner talked to the dog quietly and calmly, and it appears that Fellow knew what to do. Man and dog were tested with screens between them to avoid cueing and Fellow did well, particularly in retrieving objects. He did, however, make the occasional mistake. He would fetch an object that did not match the one described by the owner.

THE EFFECT OF MISSING TEETH

Sixty years later, a British psychologist re-examined Fellow's story. He discovered that Fellow had a couple of teeth missing from one side, as a result of which the dog found it difficult to pick up objects that were placed flat on the floor. So, when given the command to fetch an object, he carried out the task successfully if it was standing upright, but avoided it and picked up something else if it was lying flat. Likewise, if a brush was lying with the bristles upwards and therefore liable to spike him in the nose he declined to fetch it, but if the bristles faced downwards he complied with the command. Fellow had shown that he not only understood the words of his master, but also demonstrated that he possessed a kind of intelligence that had hitherto been denied to dogs.

Intelligence has been likened by some researchers to flexibility, an ability to change behaviour in response to changes in the environment. Fellow showed flexibility. He had acquired a detailed image of his world based on experience, and that accumulated knowledge gave him a view of reality. He was then able to incorporate new knowledge and to behave appropriately to changes in reality. In other words, he demonstrated some degree of intelligence. What was missing at the time Fellow lived was a way in which to measure that intelligence.

In 1911, an American psychologist called Edward Lee Thorndike devised some tests that threw light on animal intelligence. He was testing an animal's ability to learn. In order to behave appropriately, animals must have information about the world in which they live. An eagle must know how to catch and kill a rabbit, but it must also know that a rabbit is good to eat. Learning from the example of other eagles or from its own experience is one way in which an eagle obtains this knowledge. Of course, not all the information an animal requires to survive is learned. Some is inherited, though Thorndike was interested in the learned component.

He placed a variety of animals from fishes to monkeys in what he called 'puzzle boxes' and watched to see if they could learn to get out. A domestic cat, for instance, was placed in a cage from which it could emerge only if it pushed a lever or pulled a piece of string. After a long period of stumbling about, the cat discovered the means of escape, but purely by chance. Thorndike concluded that the cat, like other animals, learns by trial and error rather than by developing any 'insight'.

A person is said to have insight when he or she has contemplated a problem and then suddenly spots the solution. It is a purely mental process and is regarded as the highest form of learning, something that was once considered to be firmly in the domain of humans and not of animals.

Between 1913 and 1920, an Estonian psychologist, Wolfgang Köhler, who had found himself isolated in the Prussian Academy of Sciences on the Canary Islands during the First World War, conducted some tests with captive chimpanzees. In one experiment a bunch of bananas was hung above the chimpanzees' enclosure. The chimps could see the bananas but they were placed well out of reach. Köhler then gave the chimps some empty boxes and watched to see what would happen. The chimps sat around for some time. They looked at the bananas and seemed to look thoughtfully at the boxes. Eventually something seemed to click, and the chimps began to pile the boxes one on top of the other in order to reach the fruit. Köhler concluded that the chimps had identified the problem and arrived at a solution using their own thought processes. They had shown, Köhler thought, insight.

Later, zookeepers pointed out that chimpanzees often play by piling boxes on top of each other, and that Köhler's chimps may have reached their solution unintentionally. In addition, it was found that both the boxes and the bananas had

PROBLEM SOLVERS *The Estonian psychologist Wolfgang Köhler tested the ability of chimpanzees to solve problems.*

to be in the chimps' field of view before they would perform well. If the boxes and bananas were widely separated, the chimps apparently lost their insight and resorted to ineffective trial and error in order to get at the food.

HOW TO ASSESS INTELLIGENCE

Since those early learning experiments, scientists have devised many ways of testing an animal's ability to reason. The simplest have been 'conditioning' experiments that showed an animal could appreciate that one event follows another in time, such as a dog being fed every time a bell is rung. These tests have revealed that 'higher' animals – fish, amphibians, reptiles, birds and mammals – are able to complete the tasks successfully, but they have given very little information about whether one animal is more intelligent than another. Goldfish and sharks, for example, have done just as well as rats, dogs and chimpanzees.

Some tests, known as 'discrimination tests', have revealed more. In one simple experiment, animals were set a series of similar problems and were invited to identify the similarity; if they could, they received a reward. The way it worked was simple. A piece of food was hidden under one of two objects: say, always under the left-hand object. The animal had to learn always to look under the objects on the left in order to obtain the reward. Having gained that knowledge, the animal was tested again. The food was placed under different types of object, but always under the left one. The time taken by the animal to look under the left-hand object was some measure of how intelligent it was.

Here again the scientists had to be careful about the way in which they interpreted their results. Monkeys, after all, are better able to lift things than, say, rats. They also have better eyesight. Monkeys learn visual tasks more quickly, but rats do better in smelling tests because rats have a better sense of smell.

Animals have so many specialised abilities that it is impossible to reach any general conclusion about their intelligence. Another test illustrates the problem. In an experiment, an animal is prevented from reaching a food reward by a barrier it has to go round. A chicken separated from its food by a wire fence continually tries to break through and only finds its way around by chance. A dog, not surprisingly, discovers a route relatively quickly. The big surprise is the chameleon, an animal not noted for its intelligence. It is particularly adept at solving spatial problems.

A chameleon can look in two directions at once. Its turret-like eyes, set on either side of its head, move independently of each other. In the wild, this slow-moving reptile is able to watch for flying insects approaching from above and behind and at the same time look for those that have settled on a leaf in front. But when it spots a particularly appetising meal, both eyes swivel on to the target and, like a stereoscopic range finder, enable the chameleon to judge its distance and direction. If it is within range, the chameleon shoots out its long sticky tongue and captures the prey.

CLEVER CHAMELEON *The chameleon is remarkably 'clever' in working out how to home in on its target.*

If a resting insect is out of range on a neighbouring branch, say, the chameleon may need to make a detour. And even though the target may be temporarily out of sight, this resourceful predator will remember its position and approach from the right direction until it is close enough to use its formidable weapon. In laboratory tests, therefore, this aptitude for solving spatial problems ensures the chameleon a high score, but it provides little information about how clever it is.

Animals learn how to complete a task by trying out all sorts of behaviour, using the trial-and-error principle to discard those that do not work. The general feeling among scientists is that the more intelligent an animal is, the fewer tries it needs, since it will find the solution quickly, even immediately.

TREE-OF-LIFE RANKING

Another measure of animal intelligence often suggested is an animal's status on the tree of life. A high-ranking mammal, such as the chimpanzee or dolphin, is thought to be more intelligent than, say, a bird. But birds and mammals evolved from ancient reptilian ancestors many millions of years ago, long before the dinosaurs appeared on Earth. They have evolved over the same great span of time to develop into the animals we see today. It should come as no surprise, then, to find an African grey parrot called Alex doing just as well in human-animal communication experiments as a bottle-nosed dolphin or a chimpanzee.

And then there is the concept of 'self'. In one test a dot of bright paint was daubed on the head of a sleeping chimpanzee. When the chimp woke up, it was presented with a mirror. Without hesitation the

IN THE WILD *Captive chimpanzees returned to the wild have to be taught how to survive. Wild chimps learn these skills from parents and friends.*

animal peered into the mirror, put its hand to its head and started to scratch at the paint. This showed that the animal appreciated the difference between itself and other individuals – in other words, that it was self-aware. Monkeys fail the test. Instead, they threaten their image, and even look behind the mirror, searching for the 'rival' they believe to be on the other side. Elephants have been presented with jumbo-sized mirrors, but they walk straight through them. This could indicate a simple inability to recognise mirrors or that monkeys and elephants are just not aware of themselves. Nor is it certain that an awareness of itself in a mirror implies that a chimpanzee has greater intellectual powers.

There are clearly more questions than answers in this complicated field. In particular, why should chimpanzees be able to perform in these ways at all? Why does a chimpanzee have the ability to build stairways from boxes or recognise itself in a mirror when it would never meet such challenges in everyday life? Why is it seemingly so clever, when it is unlikely to need such intelligence in the wild?

Perhaps chimpanzees do need to solve problems in emergencies in order to find new foods or communicate with their fel-

THE ARTIST'S LIFE *This chimp in a Kenyan sanctuary has shown an interest in painting.*

lows. Some experiments carried out by the psychologist Emil Menzel with captive chimpanzees hint at the way in which this apparently high degree of intelligence may be needed in the wild. The tests were carried out in a large field with half a dozen young chimpanzees. Menzel took out one or two at a time, showed them a pile of food hidden under a bush in the field, and then returned them to the group.

The youngsters were loath to venture into the field, and certainly would not go out alone. The only way they could muster up enough courage was to go as a group.

This is why the scouts – the chimps who had already been shown the food – had somehow to communicate to the others that there was something 'out there' that made the risk of a journey into the unknown worth their while.

If the scouts were dominant animals, they went out into the field and the others followed. If the scouts were subordinates they pulled the fur of the others and looked beseechingly towards the food. If ignored, they threw tantrums. Menzel then complicated the experiment. He showed the chimps two piles of food, one larger

than the other. The group decided unanimously to visit the larger pile every time.

In a further series of experiments, Menzel introduced his captive troupe to unpleasant objects, such as snakes. Chimpanzees are terrified of snakes, and so he hid a rubber snake under some leaves in the field, showed one chimp the spot, and then returned this chimp to the others. This time they behaved quite differently. They crept up with hair-bristling, fear grins on their faces, slapped their hands on the leaves until the toy was uncovered, and then beat it to 'death'. Menzel went even further. He showed a chimp a snake hidden under leaves, but after the chimp had been returned to its companions, took the snake away. The group's reaction was even more dramatic. As before, they approached the place where the snake had been hidden, discovered it was not there, and then searched systematically up and down the entire field until satisfied that the danger had gone.

Menzel's chimpanzees had somehow told each other that there was food worth retrieving or a dangerous object out there. It is possible, then, that chimpanzees have reached an evolutionary stage at which they have the capacity to think ahead and make a mental image of something that is not readily visible. This is surely an intelligent thing to do. The experiments, albeit with captive animals, have provided a window into the chimpanzee mind, but it is in their true, wild home that the real clues are to be found.

LIFE IN THE WILD

Chimpanzee researchers such as the British Jane Goodall at Gombe, East Africa, have begun to reveal the private life of the chimpanzee. They have seen chimpanzees hunting together with a precision that would be the envy of any military strategist. They have observed individuals wielding sticks as weapons and watched young

chimpanzees learning from their parents how to crack hard nuts using rock tools.

Their studies are a reminder that all of life on Earth has evolved to fill a particular niche. Nature has given every creature the wherewithal to survive and thrive. Each has its own place in which it can feed and reproduce. Its brain and body have been honed to perfection over millions of years. Imagine how difficult it must be to unravel those evolutionary twists and turns in order to distinguish an animal's true intellectual abilities. It is even harder, when one realises that most intelligence tests have been tried out on animals in captivity, isolated, in cages, compounds and laboratories, from their normal ways of life.

So it is to an animal's natural home that one must turn to make some sense of its needs and desires, and here there are some remarkable tales of what on the surface appears to be highly intelligent behaviour. Wild rats, for example, are incredibly difficult to catch or kill. They are suspicious of anything 'new' in their environment. They will approach a poisoned bait and sniff it, but they will only eat a

small quantity. If they feel unwell, they avoid that kind of bait in future.

The rat may offer a clue about why some animals appear more intelligent than others. The rat, like humans, is a generalist and a survivor. In eking out a living in the sewers of London or the fields of Kent, it must cope with every eventuality that nature throws at it. It has, for example, built up a close relationship with people, adapting quickly to different kinds of human foods, learning to raid crops and stores, and to avoid being caught.

Many other animals, from koalas in Australia to the ground-dwelling kakapo parrot in New Zealand, are more focused in their behaviour. They are specialists. They live in a particular environment that changes little, apart from seasonal changes in the weather, foraging for the same foods and lodging in the same places. They have

little need to adapt to changing circumstances, and consequently show very few outward signs of what might be called intelligent behaviour. That is not to say they are not intelligent: it is just that there are few obvious signs of it during their everyday lives.

There are a few anomalies, too. The dolphin is a specialist, with a regular daily pattern of foraging and feeding, but it has a large brain and appears to behave intelligently in captivity . . . or does it? The dolphin has a powerful echolocation system with which it interrogates its watery environment. It produces very high-frequency sounds that it bounces off objects in the water. The returning echoes indicate to the dolphin whether the object is dead or alive, fast or slow, friend or foe. There is even some evidence that it can

detect the 'mood' of another dolphin from changes in the companion's physiology, a racing heart, tense muscles or variations in skin conductivity. Blindfolded, it can locate and identify an object the size of an tangerine from a distance of 123 yd (113 m). This remarkable sound system requires considerable brain power.

The dolphin's large brain, then, may have little to do with superintelligence. Rather, it is an enormous auditory control centre, amazing in itself, but not an organ associated with higher thought processes. The dolphin's performance in a marine circus may be no more proof of intelligent behaviour than that shown by a performing dog. Despite years of testing in captivity the results are still inconclusive.

So, again, we must turn to the wild for answers to our questions. In order to

discover just how intelligent a chimpanzee, a rat or a dolphin really is and how it makes use of that intelligence, it must be tested against the forces in its wild, natural home. Whether we consider it intelligent or not also depends on the way we define and measure intelligence, criteria still under debate in the scientific community. If we consider intelligence as the general ability to learn, then many animals are remarkably intelligent. Exploring, reasoning, solving problems, imitating, remembering – all can be regarded as features of intelligence. Indeed, from their earliest days, animals are enrolled in the school of life.

DOLPHIN TRICKS *Bottle-nosed dolphins reveal some intelligent behaviour in the wild, as well as performing tricks in captivity.*

THE SCHOOL OF LIFE

1

LEARNING FROM MOTHER
*A lion cub's first lessons
are with its mother.*

LIKE HUMAN CHILDREN, MANY YOUNG ANIMALS HAVE TO GO TO SCHOOL. AN ANIMAL'S VERY SURVIVAL DEPENDS ON WHAT IT LEARNS DURING ITS FORMATIVE YEARS, AND ON HOW WELL IT LEARNS IT. IN ADDITION TO INSTINCT — THE INNATE KNOWLEDGE AN ANIMAL INHERITS FROM ITS PARENTS — IT MUST ACQUIRE NEW INFORMATION BY LEARNING FROM THE EXAMPLE OF ITS PARENTS AND OTHER ADULTS, OR BY PLAYING WITH OTHERS OF ITS OWN AGE, OR FROM ITS OWN EXPERIENCES. ONLY WITH THIS EXTRA KNOWLEDGE WILL THE ANIMAL BE ABLE TO MEET THE ESSENTIAL REQUIREMENTS FOR ITS SURVIVAL: A SAFE PLACE TO LIVE, AMPLE FOOD TO EAT, AND A PARTNER TO PERPETUATE ITS GENES.

LEARNING TOGETHER *Burchell's
zebras are social animals.*

ATTENTIVE TEACHERS

Animal mothers – in common with human mothers – tend to bear the brunt when it comes to bringing up baby. In fact, the education of their offspring may start even before the actual birth or hatching.

Does a blackbird inherit the notes and melody with which it greets spring mornings, or has it learned its song? Does a honeybee know instinctively where it can find a patch of nectar-rich flowers, or has it learned the way to go? Does a lion on the savannahs of Africa automatically know which wildebeest to chase, or has it learned by experience which victim to choose?

In short, does an animal behave the way it does because it has inherited the instructions – a kind of blueprint for life contained in every cell of its body? Or does it learn by experience and from others everything it needs to know to survive?

During the 1970s, the 'nature versus nurture' question was hotly debated by scientists and philosophers. Tempers were raised, reputations challenged, and some fiery individuals nearly came to blows. There was, of course, no simple answer. In reality, there is a delicate and often intricate interplay in animals between instinct and learning. The information an animal inherits may influence what it learns, so that it learns some things more easily or more quickly than others. Even behaviour that seems instinctive, almost automatic, can be altered, or triggered off, by a dramatic change in the environment. The tendency of humans to line up behind formidable leaders, for example, can lie dormant for long periods until a crisis hits a society.

The life of every animal, from the

simplest amoeba to creatures as complex as humans, is affected by two factors: the innate behaviour it shares with other members of the same species, and its capacity to learn from experience, gaining knowledge that will enrich and modify the patterns of behaviour predetermined by its genes.

Throughout an animal's life, instinct and learning influence each other, the resulting behaviour varying from species to species and from one individual to another. Even a creature whose behaviour seems to be purely instinctive, such as a freshwater hydra (one of the most basic of animal organisms), has the capacity to use stored information. The more complex the creature, the more information it must acquire. For those on the higher branches of the tree of life – mammals, for example – the ability to find food and shelter, to locate a partner and to find one's way about requires a long apprenticeship.

MOTHER LOVE *Mallard ducklings learn to recognise their mother's voice while still in the egg.*

The process starts at birth and continues throughout life until death. The contributions to an animal's store of knowledge come from parents, close relatives, neighbours and the everyday experiences of its life. Like human children, many young animals play games that they repeat over and over again, perfecting the movements that will become vital later in adulthood. While they are growing up they observe, copy and break new ground. Elder brothers and sisters, cousins and aunts may help with the education, and for some animals school starts even before they are born.

A MOTHER'S CALL

While a mother mallard is incubating her clutch of eggs, she talks to her unhatched offspring – and they talk back. She starts the conversation, about 17–19 days after her eggs have been laid, just when the embryo duckling's head pushes into the air space at one end of the egg. The youngsters learn the duck calls of their own species, and, more importantly, their mother's voice, some time before they hatch, and so respond to her calls as soon as they emerge.

The lesson is important, for ducklings are precocious birds. They do not remain in a protected nest but must be on the move, following their mother, right from the start. If they are not to get lost and fall prey to ever-vigilant predators, they have to know how to find mother quickly. Sound is the answer, and the sound of their mother's voice overrides any other. The sound of mother is even more important than what she looks like.

In an experiment, scientists replaced a real mother duck with a model one, and by a process known as 'imprinting' – by which chicks and ducklings form lasting attachments to creatures and even inanimate objects during their first hours of life – they fooled the newly hatched ducklings into believing that the model was their real mother. They followed the model duck

HYDRA MEMORY *Although a simple organism, the freshwater hydra still possesses a memory.*

wherever it was taken, and as long as they were fed they were happy. Then a cardboard box, painted with red and white stripes and containing a loudspeaker, was introduced into their enclosure. The mother duck's assembly call was played through the speaker and immediately the ducklings abandoned their stuffed foster mother and gathered around the box. In a second experiment, ducklings were 'imprinted' on a live, silent duck but they still preferred the box as long as it made the right sounds.

These prehatching conversations are

TURKEY CALLING

Sound is important to a turkey chick. Indeed, its very survival can depend on its voice, because if a mother turkey cannot hear her chick's call she will kill it. In an experiment, naturalists observed a deaf turkey hen who had laid some eggs. She sat and incubated them in the normal way, but when the chicks hatched and started to run around she was unable to recognise them as her own and tried to kill them. Although she could see her chicks, she needed to be able to hear the contact call to suppress her natural aggression.

vital in the wild. In a test carried out on a colony of ring-billed gulls living along Washington state's Pacific shoreline, one clutch of eggs was exposed to the sound of maternal feeding calls, while another clutch was incubated in silence. After hatching, the chicks that had heard their

DICING WITH DEATH *A chick lost in a gull colony may be killed if it cannot locate its parent's call.*

the supply of mother's milk in the case of a mammal. But in an animal's natural home it must also quickly establish what is good and bad for its survival. Learning about the right foods to eat is fundamental.

The rare mountain gorillas of Rwanda, Uganda and Zaire spend about a third of their time eating. They are surrounded by hundreds of different plants, some good, others not so palatable, and a young gorilla must learn which is which.

Its first contact with solid food is at about three months. It may lie on its mother's stomach, picking up and tasting the scraps of food she has dropped. Sometimes it snatches pieces from her hands or takes them from her mouth. She rarely protests, allowing her youngster to taste the plants that will make up a daily diet for the rest of its life. The young gorilla is usually weaned by the time it is eight months old but may continue to feed at the breast until it is 18 months. By this time, it will have sampled and learned to recognise most of the 58 or so plants, including bamboo shoots, giant nettles, thistles and wild celery, that gorillas like to eat. It makes a gastronomic voyage of discovery under the watchful eye of its mother.

mother's call pecked at her beak in the normal way, which encouraged her to regurgitate a predigested fish stew. The other group did not peck at their mother, and would not have been able to feed. Without that key piece of knowledge, they would normally have died.

Hearing a mother's calls while still in the egg is thought to have additional survival value. Ring-billed gulls live in dense colonies where a wandering chick is just as likely to be attacked and killed by a highly territorial neighbour of the same species as by a predator. So, when a parent returns to the nest after a feeding excursion both chick and parent call frantically to each other. The parent only knows where to search by listening for the sound of its offspring. Likewise, the chick only responds to its own parent's call. As soon as a parent hears the cry of its chick, it gives a long 'mewing' call and the hungry youngster runs back to the nest.

The prospect of food encourages this rapid return – the chick has learned to associate the call with a meal. At the

same time, it knows exactly which call to respond to. This saves its life – provided that it successfully negotiates the corridor of stabbing bills back to its nest. It had acquired this knowledge while in its egg.

LEARNING WHAT TO EAT

There comes a time when an animal must learn to feed itself. Having successfully entered the world, it is first provided for by its mother – whether its food is brought to it as in the case of a bird, or comes from

'IMPRINTING' — AN ATTACHMENT TO MOTHER

Shortly after hatching from its egg, a chick or duckling is sensitive to the shape of the first thing it sees, usually its mother. This is the time – no more than a few hours – when the newly hatched bird forms a lasting attachment to its parent in a process known as 'imprinting'. It learns her principal characteristics, and those of its own species, and thus picks up the cues for it to develop normal social and sexual behaviour.

Newly hatched birds can, however,

MOTHER'S LEAD *Peregrine chicks may view a human nursemaid as 'mother'.*

imprint on anything they see, from a ball to a person, and the imprinting can last all their life. Confused turkeys that have been imprinted on people, for example, mix with other turkeys but prefer the company of humans. Imprinting is a curious form of learning in that no obvious reward is needed to reinforce it – although in the wild a youngster's mother is the source of food and protection. Other animals imprint on the odour of the nest, the flavour of their mother's milk and the sounds she makes.

For some animals, notably those that eat other animals – carnivores – establishing the identity of food is only the start of the learning process. The young animal also has to learn where the food is most likely to be found, and, having discovered that, to work out how to prevent it from getting away. Polecats start 'predator school' even before their eyes open at 24 days old, when their mother presents them with their first solid food. She brings dead prey, such as small rodents, to the nest – a hole under a tree or an old rabbit burrow – and encourages her young ones to lick it. By 28 days they can move towards the food she has brought for them and can take their first bite. From then on they greet their mother's return with begging calls until they are weaned at six weeks.

The third step of predatory development coincides with the young polecats' first forays from the nest. They begin to act aggressively towards each other, snarling and snatching prey. It is time for the mother to introduce them to the real feast of life. She places a dead mouse or vole in front of them and then, just as they are about to take a bite, she takes it away. She puts it back, then snatches it away again, using the game to entice her youngsters to reproduce the complete hunting sequence – pursuit, capture and kill – that will enable them eventually to feed without help. The pattern is repeated time and time again until the young hunters are ready for the real thing – a living creature that they must stop and kill for themselves.

At about eight weeks old, their movements are sufficiently advanced for the mother to bring them live prey. First, they identify the victim's smell and the texture of its fur. Having

established that it is fair game, they pursue, capture and kill. At first, they try clumsy bites to the back, which means that the victim takes some time to die – nature can be very cruel. But gradually they perfect their killing technique until finally they are able to deliver the *coup de grâce* with one bite to the neck. Having completed their apprenticeship, they are ready to leave their mother and fend for themselves.

DOLPHIN FAMILY LIFE

Land mammals have to learn how to walk, run, turn this way and that and chase before they can tackle prey. But their aquatic relatives, from whales and dolphins that live permanently in the sea to otters and seals that venture on to land, must learn a whole gamut of skills before they are ready to hunt.

The newborn dolphin must first learn to breathe. Seconds after its birth, the mother and her family helpers watch

EARLY LEARNING *Polecats begin to learn about hunting even before their eyes are open.*

carefully to see if the calf can reach the surface on its own. Mother and calf talk to each other, the calf producing unsure whistling sounds. If it is having difficulties, the mother and helpers nudge it gently to the surface where it can take its first vital, life-giving breath.

NATURE'S BOUNTY *Mountain gorillas have to discover which foods are good to eat.*

A FOX CUB'S FIRST HUNT

Fox cubs have to learn how to hunt. On one occasion, David MacDonald, a fox researcher based at Oxford in England, watched a vixen teach a cub how to deal with earthworms. The boisterous youngster had mastered the 'mouse-jump' – jumping high into the air so as to fall with the front paws on the prey – but had failed to realise that it was a totally inappropriate way in which to catch worms. The female helped her pupil by showing it the simpler and more effective technique of gently using the teeth to pull the worm out of its hole without breaking it. The fox cub, being a good pupil, quickly understood its mistake and used this method. It was duly rewarded with a big worm. Fox cubs have to learn their lessons well, for when older each will need over 1 lb (450 g) of food a day.

FOX HUNTING *Red fox cubs learn from mother how to find and catch their food.*

Breathing for these animals is not automatic; it is a conscious activity over which they have some degree of control. The young dolphin must learn where and when to take a breath. It learns to exhale and inhale in 0.3 seconds and to surface once or twice every minute. Eventually, it will be able to hold its breath for about seven minutes at a time. During the training period, mother and calf squeak and burp at each other constantly. Who is to say that the mother is not teaching her offspring the lore of the sea?

RELUCTANT SWIMMERS

Among young European otters, on the other hand, a few just do not like the water. Some reluctant pupils will do all they can to avoid a ducking, for they are born and raised on land and that is where they want to stay. Most behave as otters should behave and are led into the water without fuss. But some are instinctively afraid of water, and so their mother has to carry or drag them in and teach them how to swim.

Once in the sea or river they flap about, swallowing mouthfuls of water. At the slightest opportunity they make for the shore, where the mother throws them straight back in. Sometimes she takes a youngster on her back and swims out to deeper water where the hesitant swimmer has two choices: sink or swim. Inevitably they swim, and once waterborne the promise of a plump crayfish entices them out to still deeper water for fishing lessons.

In reality, they cannot sink, for the young ones' fluffy coats trap too much air. Diving is difficult at first, but as they grow older their fur becomes slicker and traps less air. After a few weeks they can dive below, and by four months they can catch their own food. But they still have a lot to learn about the finer skills of hunting. Each night they follow their mother on her journeys until eventually they leave home and hunt for themselves.

SEAL SCHOOL

Grey seal pups are more adventurous. Although most will not venture into water for several weeks after being born, they are capable of swimming within 24 hours of their birth, and baby seals living along the

IN AT THE DEEP END *A grey seal pup may go swimming with its mother before it is a day old.*

shores of south-west Wales swim before the end of their first day.

As they grow bigger they take their swimming lessons more seriously, at first flapping awkwardly with their fore flippers like a dog paddling, but later propelling themselves with their rear flippers in the manner of adult seals. Eventually, they can swim fast enough and nimbly enough to intercept fish and catch their own food.

'WHALES' THAT LIKE TO LAND

On the shores of Possession Island in the Crozet Archipelago of the Southern Ocean, and on the equally windswept beaches of Peninsula Valdés on the Patagonian coast of Argentina, term starts at another kind of hunting school. The teachers weigh 4 tons or more and are 23 ft (7 m) long; the pupils are a third to a half that size. They are orcas or killer whales (actually a large member of the dolphin family) and they catch their prey in a remarkable way.

For most of the schools or 'pods' of orcas in the world's oceans, hunting involves trapping fish, catching seals and sea lions and harassing whales and dolphins at sea. They hunt cooperatively, each member of the pod playing its role in herding the prey. They coordinate their attack, some groups communicating with a barrage of squeaks, burps and moans.

But the Crozet and Patagonian orcas are different. They leave the water, beach themselves and snatch young seals from the shore. The hunting strategy is not only dangerous for the prey, it could also be fatal for the predator. In the sea, an orca's great bulk is supported by the water, but on land it is in danger of being suffocated and crushed by its own weight. Out of water, it risks dehydration, and to avoid these pitfalls the orcas regularly practise the manoeuvre of beaching themselves.

On beaches where there are no animals that are likely to prey on them, young

FIRST BREATH *A bottle-nosed dolphin mother nudges her baby to the surface. It has to learn to take its first breath.*

orcas and their mothers have training sessions. Mother and baby lie out 23 ft (7 m) or so offshore, facing the beach, and then rush ashore. Helped by the waves, they slide up onto the pebbles, the mother usually a little way ahead of her attentive offspring. By staying a yard or so in front, the mother can ensure that her inexperienced beach-raider returns safely to the ocean. Using wide and violent flexing movements of the trunk and tail, the mother shuffles back into the water, nudging her calf ahead of her.

Bull orcas, which are much larger and heavier than the females, only take part in these training sessions when the angle of the beach is sufficiently steep for them to squirm back into the water without too much effort. The youngsters learn quickly, and are then ready to join their parents for an assault on seal beaches.

The targets at Crozet are young elephant seals; in Patagonia they are fur seals. The orcas congregate close to the shore, ready for the attack. They hunt mainly in silence, emitting a few high-frequency echolocation clicks and the occasional squawk-like, short-distance contact call. Without warning, the characteristic black and white shape of an adult orca rides in on a large wave and surges up the beach. The weaned seal pups, surprised that their land-based haven should be invaded in this fashion, scatter noisily. The orca seizes a pup by its rear flippers, turns broadside to

GRAND OLD LADY *A powerful and experienced matriarch heads up a herd of African elephants.*

the sea and shuffles back into the surf. On the next large wave, it swims out to deeper water. But the story does not end here.

Suddenly, the seal pup is thrown into the air. It lands with a muffled splash on the surface. Then, with a loud thwack like a cricketer hitting a ball, the orca bats the seal into the air with its powerful tail. Again and again, the orca slams into its victim, like parents playing ball with their children – only the 'ball' is a living seal pup. Naturalists are still not sure why they carry out this 'game', though one suggestion is that it loosens the seal pup's skin and breaks its bones to make eating easier.

Mastery of the beaching technique ensures an easy meal in Patagonia or at Crozet. Elsewhere, orcas learn similar hunting methods. Farther south, on the fringes of the Antarctic pack ice, young orcas learn how to tip a seal from an ice

floe. A whale jumps from the water and lands with all its weight bearing down on one side of the block of ice, which then tilts, while sometimes another member of the pod lifts the block from the other side. The victim slides into the water.

The teacher in an orca playschool is not always mother. If a baby orca's mother is not particularly gifted at beaching or berg-tilting, her offspring will practise with a close relative. Led by an older female and accompanied by a large bull, all the members of an orca pod – mostly females with babies and adolescents – are related, and all take an interest in rearing the next generation. They form a protective cordon around a youngster if danger threatens.

More importantly, they teach by example the ways of killer whale life. Baby orcas born in captivity to mothers who have not learned how to raise a calf, for

example, often die. A young orca mother must learn from its own mother and from the other females in the pod how to nurse and care for her calf. Orcas, like many other 'social' mammals, need a long period of learning.

THE ELEPHANT CHILD

African elephants also live in family groups, and as with orcas the family is headed by the oldest and most respected female. She guides the herd, a group consisting of sisters and daughters with their offspring. Bulls, which lead a solitary life, only appear when a female is on heat. Babies are born after two years' gestation.

When a birth is imminent, all the members of the elephant herd take an interest, especially the females. Generally, though not always, a mother isolates herself to give birth to her enormous 265 lb (120 kg) baby, but within minutes the rest of the females gather round to inspect the newborn elephant. They support the calf when it tries to stand up, and caress and smell it with their trunks. For the first few days of its life, the calf never strays far from its mother, sheltering beneath her great bulk or hiding behind her legs.

Young females, particularly inexperienced sisters and daughters, gather around the mother and sometimes they are allowed to take care of the calf. Such baby-sitting is common and an important way in which adolescent females gain experience in calf-rearing. On one occasion a baby-sitter proved just how useful it could be. The baby of the group fell asleep, but the herd, including mother, moved off, leaving the calf peacefully slumbering under an acacia tree. Without the protection of the herd, it would have been vulnerable to an attack by lions or hyenas. Fortunately, an elder sister realised it had been left behind and went back to wake it up.

If, however, a newborn calf is the mother's first, it is she who must learn. Just as experienced sisters, aunts and grandmothers descend on the house of a human mother and her first-born, elephant helpers do the same. In fact, without their help, it is doubtful if the baby would survive

at all. A first-time mother is clumsy and does not know how to guide her calf to her teats to take its first meal.

Elephant births are rarely witnessed by scientists, since they often happen at night or among thick scrub away from prying eyes. But elephant researcher Cynthia Moss, who has studied elephants in Kenya for many years, was fortunate in observing the first few hours in the life of two elephant calves. Their start in life could not have been more different. One mother was experienced, having successfully reared several calves already. She was very calm and sure of herself. Two young females were with her and watched and learned what to do. Between mother and helpers, the newborn calf was well cared for.

The other mother was inexperienced, and so too was the helper accompanying her. There had been no birth in their family for several years and neither mother nor helper knew what to do. Deprived of

---

ELEPHANT LIFE CYCLES

A baby elephant will remain dependent on its mother, drinking her milk (through its mouth, not its trunk) for three to four years – it may even try to sneak a drink up to the age of nine. Puberty comes between 10 and 18 years old for elephants, depending on how much nourishment they find in their environment. After that, female elephants remain with the herd, while males leave to join bachelor herds. Later, the bulls live a solitary life. Some will live for 60 years, although half those born will die before they are 15 years old.

---

their normal apprenticeship, they were helpless. Desperately they tried to encourage the calf to feed but they could not guide it to the teats. Later it died.

The offspring of many social animals, particularly female offspring, remain in their family group, learning more and more about how to cope with everyday

life. Males tend to go their separate ways, although even they often form into bachelor groups, not only for mutual protection, but also to rehearse the fights they must win later in life in order to take a partner. Most other animals turn out or chase away their maturing offspring, but not all: some children remain at home.

STAYING TO MIND THE NEST

In North America, fledgling scrub jays, for example, help their parents at the nest. Scrub jays are highly territorial, defending large areas of patchy, open scrub. Parents with sons and daughters that stay behind and help to feed new generations of chicks, have more time to devote to territorial defence. And with less foraging to do themselves, the parents lose less body weight and so breed more frequently.

The helpers benefit greatly, too. Young, inexperienced birds are unable to hold a viable territory and would be poor breeders, and so they do not try. Instead, they stay to help their parents. In doing so they gain 'on the job' training, learning from their parents the best places to forage and the best ways for defending their patch. This apprenticeship also helps them to breed.

The frequent flights to and from the nest give them detailed information about the lie of the land and where the best territories are. From the relatively safe position of helper, they are better able to capitalise on any territories that become available. It pays, then, to be a helper and pupil, since the animal learns how to be a mother or father. It then successfully rears offspring of its own, which in their turn begin another cycle of learning.

LEARNING THROUGH PLAY

Play is a nearly universal form of behaviour among the young of higher animals – birds and mammals. But naturalists still know very little about it, and can only speculate about its function.

Stalking one another, chasing and escaping and then engaging in friendly combat are all games that young animals play. The games help to perfect the youngsters' skills, preparing them to hunt for prey, flee from predators and assume a place in their different societies.

At this stage, it is all make-believe. The young protagonists run even though there are no predators chasing them or prey for them to chase. They fight each other without drawing blood and make sexual advances towards one another without ever actually coupling. They repeat the games time and time again, the experiences gained gradually moulding the youngsters' patterns of behaviour until they are equipped for adulthood.

But not all changes in an animal's behaviour are the result of learning. A male puppy urinates by squatting, in the same way as a bitch, but as an adult dog it will cock its leg to perform the same function. The pup has not learned anything new in the intervening months to make it change its behaviour. The change is simply a result of reaching sexual maturity, and the significant increase in the quantity of male hormones circulating in the bloodstream. In the case of a dog, these encourage it to cock its leg.

The release of hormones, the body's chemical messengers, plays an important role in behaviour. They are secreted continuously and in precisely controlled amounts and alter an animal's desire to indulge in certain types of activity – notably, they affect the development of sexual behaviour. They also influence to some extent the urges and desires that are thought to account for much of an animal's other behaviour – its motivation or drive, for example. At an early age, the motivating drive of many of the higher animals, particularly mammals, is the desire to play.

STALKING MOTHER *A tiger cub's first 'victim' is usually its mother – in play. Later, it will progress to the real thing.*

Play is a curious type of behaviour and is still one of the great enigmas in ethology (the study of animal behaviour). What possesses a young animal, such as a lion cub or wolf cub, to chase, pounce and bite when it is neither hungry nor thirsty? Why does a zebra foal or a mountain goat kid suddenly leap into the air and bounce about so frenetically when there is no obstacle to overcome or enemy to flee? Why are the movements in play so exaggerated and repeated so many times? Is an animal simply burning off surplus energy, or does play ensure that it is at a suitable pitch of arousal and not bored? Is play 'fun', or is it purely functional?

Like many aspects of animal behaviour, there are more questions than answers, but on the basis of studies to date scientists are able to make educated guesses. The general feeling is that the purpose of play is to prepare the young animal for the activities of adult life. It is also most commonly seen in young mammals, rather than in any other group of animals.

KITTENISH PLOYS

Kittens playing on the hearth-rug are encouraged by their mother to play games that closely resemble fighting, fleeing or hunting. Crouched low on the floor, a young kitten watches its sibling. It seems to glide across the floor as its gets ready to pounce. Suddenly, it leaps on its playmate, much as it would do on a mouse. The young animal's movements are decidedly clumsy at first but they improve with practice, until the mother decides that her youngsters are ready for the real thing and she brings home an injured mouse or bird on which they can practise their hunting and killing.

In the wild, bigger cats, such as cheetah cubs, play continuously. Under the watchful eye of their mother – cheetahs are vulnerable to attack from lions, leopards and hyenas – the young litter-mates wrestle and chase in and around the family den. This 'friendly' combat can be rough but there are rarely injuries, since the cubs' claws and teeth have not yet grown sufficiently to cause serious damage. As they grow older, their agility and coordination improve and they learn to hunt together. They lie in wait for each other, chase one another, and pretend to stalk, crawling silently on their stomachs before pouncing on their playmates as though they were real prey. They also take an interest in inanimate objects, throwing leaves and sticks into the air and chasing them.

At three to four months old, the mother cheetah begins to bring back some specimens of live prey, such as baby Thomson's gazelles. These small gazelles pose little threat to the cheetah cubs, but they provide excellent sport. The mother drops the gazelle in front of her cubs and both apprentice hunters and terrified prey stare apprehensively at each other. The gazelle attempts to escape but a cub pounces, and starts playing with its victim as it would with its brothers and sisters. But then it realises that the gazelle represents food and accordingly tries to kill it. At first, the cubs chase and pounce to little avail, but their mother watches closely and prevents the prey from escaping.

At six months old, they have acquired the skills to go on a real hunt and begin to accompany their mother. Initially, they watch and wait on the sidelines, following the course of the hunt and observing the kill (again, usually Thomson's gazelle).

SPOTTED HUNTER *Like the babies of all big cats, a leopard cub learns the basics of hunting through play.*

Gradually they join in until, between the ages of one and two, they can hunt gazelles for themselves. They enter the adult world as the fastest land hunters in the world.

PREPARING FOR FLIGHT

Gazelles play, too, not to practise getting food, but to reduce the chance of appearing on the menu. The favourite game of young 'tommies' is the chase. The ability to run fast helps them to escape predators such as cheetahs and leopards, and it is reflected in their play. They start off suddenly, sprinting away quickly and chasing each other across the savannah. They practise these sudden surges of speed, perfecting their manoeuvrability, toning up their muscles and increasing their lung capacity.

They also learn when to flee and what from. Young gazelles learn the shape and likely movements of their enemies and leave sufficient fleeing distance to ensure a successful escape. Jackals may come as close as $5\frac{1}{2}$ yd (5 m) without a gazelle moving, whereas it will take flight if a hyena comes within 450 to 550 yd (400 to 500 m). Gazelles learn the precise moment

PLAYTIME AND A GAZELLE
A young cheetah plays with a live gazelle brought home by its mother.

to run in order to save precious energy. And if taken unawares by a stealthy cheetah that remains hidden until the very last moment before attacking, there is still a chance to put some distance between the pursuer and the pursued. The cheetah, though faster over a short distance, will give up the chase after 215 yd (200 m), due to overheating. If a gazelle is able to outrun and outmanoeuvre it for more than half a minute, it will probably escape.

Play has other functions besides preparing an animal for fight or flight. Social play prepares it for the battle to establish its rightful place within its group. A gazelle fawn, for example, will first race about to increase its capacity for endurance, speed and strength – preparation for escape – but will later switch to social games. These teach it about the social environment in which it will have to

---

REHEARSING FOR LIFE

One purpose of play is to equip animals for 'social' life. But animal games such as play-fighting and chasing may also be an individual's attempt to gain other advantages in future life. A play-fight, for instance, may well be a serious rehearsal for occasions when a real fight will be all-important in a male animal's attempt to win a female. To support this notion, observations of rhesus monkeys have shown that juvenile males play-fight more frequently than young females. Similarly, play-chasing is an individual's rehearsal for avoiding predators.

---

live as an adult. Similarly, zebra foals must prepare for a hectic social life.

A zebra stallion surrounds himself with several mares and their young. Each female has its particular place in the group, the dominant female always leading a single-file procession. A hierarchy based on age is also established among the foals.

The stallion brings up the rear, ready to intervene at the least sign of danger. Young females remain in their family group, but young males leave at about three years old to form boisterous bands of three or four bachelors. The comrades stay together for a couple of years before each sets off alone to conquer its own harem. During the two years, they prepare themselves for the hard and demanding life that lies ahead.

For days on end, adolescent males test their strength in games resembling the fights that in adulthood will pit them against each other – fights for the right to mate. The rules are precise: the young adversaries circle each other warily, first trying to nibble one another's legs. The game becomes more serious when they rear up on their hind legs and attempt to bite the neck or nape. Hoof kicks are allowed, but these fights rarely lead to injuries. The fighters measure their strength, learn to ward off blows and, if faced with an overwhelming opponent, surrender and back down. In these practice bouts, a hierarchy is established, with an overall winner becoming dominant over the other young stallions in the group. When the great day comes, each young pretender heads out onto the savannah and challenges resident stallions for their mares. A

successful combatant will gather a harem of young mares. Less powerful males sometimes willingly associate with even weaker males, the latter's function being to help to ward off any competition.

Curiously, like a human class system, inheritance of rank plays an important role in establishing a young animal's social status. Zebra foals whose mothers occupy high rank are predisposed to great things. In the earliest strength-testing games, they dominate proceedings and will continue to do so for the rest of their lives. They are not necessarily stronger than their fellows, but seem to have inherited the status that belonged to their mothers. Who would have guessed, watching a large herd of apparently indistinguishable black and white zebras, that some individuals are more equal than others?

LIFE IN THE WOLF PACK

Social status aside, play seems most common in animals that are 'adaptable' – that is, creatures which have not been born with all the information necessary for their survival. They do not have, for instance, the innate instructions that tell them how to react to other animals in their group, but must learn how to adjust. During the early periods of their lives, animals like these are protected and fed while they assimilate information and practise vital skills. In a well-ordered society such as that of wolves, learning through play and example is essential if the discipline of the pack, and therefore its ability to hunt cooperatively, is to be maintained. Each wolf depends on the others in the pack for its own survival and therefore each new wolf cub learns its place in the hierarchy and the role it must play.

A wolf pack consists of an 'alpha' pair – the dominant male and female, who are partners for life – and a supporting cast that varies from 7 to 20 individuals depending on food availability. Cohesion in the pack is maintained by a complex signalling system of sounds and scents, as well as facial grimaces, tail movements, raised hackles, stiff legs and other forms of body language. At breeding time, the social calm is broken with a bout of serious fighting to resolve who the 'top dogs' are. Once the dominant pair has been established or re-established, peace is restored and the hierarchy fixed for several months; it is in this atmosphere of apparent harmony that the cubs are born.

They are born blind and helpless in late winter, but after a month they emerge from the den and their education begins. At first they play rough-and-tumble games together. At two to three months old their teeth are well formed and their jaws strong enough to give powerful bites. They begin to appreciate the meaning of the signals that will be important to them in later life, and the social graces they must perfect: they learn, for instance, that biting a playmate too hard leads to being bitten back.

They practise hunting skills. A young cub will suddenly attack a playmate with a single lightning strike. Alternatively, it will creep forward, low and slow, fixing its eyes on its intended victim, and then make a dash, leaping in an exaggerated fashion and landing on all fours beside its startled fellow. In one variation of this chasing game, a cub may finish its attack with a zigzag movement of its head – an invitation to its playmate to join in a play-fight. Another game is to lie almost flat on the

ground with forelegs outstretched and eyes open wide, the only movement coming from the tail and hindquarters – a challenge for another cub to give chase.

Even in these first games, different cubs act out the different roles of hunter and hunted. The one playing the hunter role shows signs of aggression and the other, with tail between its legs and ears

THE RIGHT TO A MATE *Young Burchell's zebra stallions practise fighting for the right to acquire a herd of females.*

flattened, plays the part of the less dominant animal. In an instant the tables are turned, and a cub standing its ground signals that the pursuer is about to be

WOLF AND DOLPHIN *Wolf cubs learn the pack's ways by watching their elders and by playing. Dolphins (opposite) perform tricks they have learned from humans.*

pursued. Opening the mouth without baring the teeth indicates that it is just play.

When the cubs are more than a month old, other members of the pack begin to take on teaching duties. They bring prey back to the den, showing the young the kinds of creatures that are good to eat. Gradually the cubs will learn to capture, kill and eat without being hurt. They also begin to explore the ground around the den, looking for food of their own. Even at four weeks, a young cub will not hesitate to chase a rat, pinning it to the ground.

Once the rat is captured, the cub pummels and smells it, the investigation ending abruptly with a clumsy bite at the creature's abdomen. Then, not yet convinced that it is dead, the cub seizes the rat by the nape of the neck and shakes it vigorously. It takes the carcass to a quiet corner, away from its litter-mates, where it throws it into the air, pushes it around with its nose, dismembers it, bites it, kicks it and eventually gets around to eating it. A few days and several corpses later, the cub will snatch any prey it comes across, give it a single bite and a quick shake and devour the body – all within 20 seconds.

THE RULES OF THE HUNT

In the meantime, relations with its playmates contribute to the cub's understanding of pack rules. They also build up a hierarchy amongst the new generation, essential for future peace and stability within the pack. During their games, the cubs practise skills that will be important when they eventually go hunting with the adults and help to bring down large prey such as moose, American elk and caribou or reindeer. They learn to bite at legs, flanks and shoulders.

During their first year, the young wolves accompany the rest of the pack, watching and learning how to select the right prey and how to coordinate an attack. A young wolf must learn when to hunt and when to give up. If a quarry is too fast or too dangerous to attack – for example, a large, fit moose at bay – the pack aborts the attack and saves energy. A small pack of young, inexperienced wolves who had split from a large pack, were once seen to surround a moose for several days

SQUIRREL MONKEY SOCIETY

Groups of primates that appear not to indulge in much play also tend to have less well-developed social relations. Researchers John and Janice Baldwin were able to record this in populations of squirrel monkeys in South America.

Those monkeys living in dry forest areas where food is in short supply rarely played games with each other. Equally notable was that social interactions between members of a troop were less numerous. The animals were probably too intent on finding food, with little time for frivolous behaviour. This left them somewhat retarded socially.

Even so, group cohesion remained intact and the members of the group somehow established a hierarchy. Play, it seems, is not absolutely necessary for establishing basic social structures.

In the humid forests where food is plentiful the young squirrel monkeys played much more frequently and, in adult life, they interacted more often with the other members of their group. This second study suggested that play is not essential for young primates, but is still important for their social development. It is the way they test the responses of their elders, learn how best to approach them and to approach other members of the troop.

NO PLAY, NO GRACE *Squirrel monkeys that are deprived of an adequate supply of food do not play. As a result, they are socially 'lacking' when they become adults.*

until they realised that there were too few of them to launch a successful attack. They had learned the hard way. It is a long and complex apprenticeship, so that a wolf cub does not reach adulthood until it is two years old.

When animals come of age, play or play-like behaviour does not necessarily stop. Adult chimpanzees will punch holes

NATURE'S ENIGMA *Breaching humpback whales may be playing boisterously or communicating with distant relatives.*

in leaves and peer through; adult domestic cats will continue to pat and chase balls of knitting wool or, when full after a meal, will 'toy' with a captured mouse. Gorillas play games in which they 'take turns' at various activities, and rhesus macaques turn upside down and leer through their legs at other members of the troop.

Dolphins and porpoises have also been seen to play. Indeed, play seems to be an important part of dolphin life. Both adults and young surf on breaking waves or ride the bow waves of ships or fast boats, apparently getting themselves a free ride.

Such behaviour seems to have arisen from riding the pressure waves that precede large baleen whales.

On several occasions people watching dolphins riding the bow wave of their boat have been deliberately splashed by the joy-riders. Dolphins also play with objects floating in the water, including feathers, seaweed and pieces of driftwood, tossing them up in the air and carrying them along on the snout. They have even been seen to leap out and chase butterflies flying over-head. None of this seems to serve any useful purpose: it is simply fun.

BIRDS AT PLAY — PREPARING FOR ADULTHOOD

Play is not restricted to mammals – birds play, too. As with mammals, play helps them to develop appropriate feeding and social behaviour, and includes chasing and fleeing, mock fighting, nose-diving other birds and somersaulting in the water. In one extraordinary case, a pet raven repeatedly threw a rubber ball high into the air and caught it again.

Young frigate birds swoop down to the sea where they pick up and then drop leaves and other floating objects, practising, no doubt, for the times they will pluck food from the surface. Rooks tumble through the air, and ravens drop and catch sprigs of heather over and over again. Noisy parties of Adélie penguins ride blocks of ice in fast-flowing currents and tide races in a game known as 'rafting'. When the raft runs aground, they all hop off, swim back to the start, and take another ride on a fresh ice floe.

SKYDIVES *Alpine choughs drop and roll through the air in a mock fight.*

Similarly, killer whales or orcas have been seen racing up and down, swimming belly up with bunches of seaweed in the mouth or dragging long strands of giant kelp about on their flippers and flukes. Young orcas on the Pacific coast of North America sometimes chase Dall's porpoises and harbour porpoises. But the porpoises remain in the area, which seems to indicate that the chase is a part of the killer whales' playfulness rather than unsuccessful hunting.

The bays of the Peninsula Valdés in Argentina are where several species of sea mammals go to breed. Here, giant southern right whales play with the wind. As the wind rises and the waves get larger, the whales' activity increases. They stand on their heads in the shallow water, push their tail flukes in the air and, quite literally, sail with the wind. Then they swim back to the starting point and do it again . . . and again. They also hurl their 40 ton bodies into the air and crash back into the water with an enormous 'thwack' and a mountain of spray – behaviour that is thought to indicate to other whales where they are located and how they are.

Some of this play has recognisable value in teaching the animal about survival. A right whale calf circles its mother and moves back and forth, but always remains close to her. Mother and calf indulge in joint sessions of flipper and tail-slapping, which will help the calf to defend itself against killer whales when it is older.

In captivity, small whales and dolphins invent all manner of games, playing with any object they find in their tank. Two entertaining bottle-nosed dolphins were once seen to tease and chase a moray eel. The eel escaped into a crevice but the dolphins would not give up that easily. Instead, one of them went to fetch a spiny scorpion fish and pushed it into the gap. The unfortunate eel was thus forced out of its retreat and the dolphins were able to continue their game.

On another occasion, a young dolphin confused communication researchers by resting on the bottom of its tank, blowing bubbles. It was playing with its own sound-producing apparatus to see just how many different sounds it could make.

GAINING EXPERIENCE

Curiosity, adventure and discovery – these enable a young animal to add its own experiences of life to the information it already possesses: information it learned from others or inherited from its parents.

Learning by example from friends and relatives and learning by play are just two ways in which a new generation of animals can obtain the knowledge it needs for survival. There is a third way: learning by experience.

To get on in the wild, just as in human society, there is no substitute for experience. Young animals discover life's pitfalls, learn from their mistakes or successes, and remember them in order to do better next time. A young mountain lion or puma encountering its first skunk may well get an eyeful of foul-smelling chemicals and will avoid such contact for ever after. An intelligent animal's curiosity may lead it to make great discoveries, ones that will be copied by others in its group. And for a young mammal like the chick in its egg, that experience can begin before it is born.

An unborn human child, for example, responds to all kinds of stimuli. It can hear the sounds made by its mother's body when she is eating, drinking, breathing and speaking and it can hear extraneous noises, too. An unborn baby will shift if it hears a harsh sound, such as the jangling of

keys. The mother's voice has a more soothing effect. Human babies, like other mammals, have a womb with a view – a sound view, that is, and their sound experiences in the womb have an influence on their behaviour once they are born.

Human infants just three days old are able to distinguish their mother's voice. In one test, babies were given artificial teats to suck. If they sucked at a particular rate, the researchers played a recording of the mother's voice reading a story. Sucking at a different rate switched on a different female voice reading the same story. Out of ten babies tested, eight quickly got the hang of it and called up their own mother; in some cases it took only ten minutes for the baby to learn the sucking pattern. If the pattern was changed the babies rapidly adapted, changing their sucking rate in order to listen to their mother's voice. As the babies were less than three days old, they had experienced

SKUNK WARNING SIGNALS *The posture and black and white 'warning' colours of a hooded skunk warn a pair of raccoons that it is about to spray.*

only a few hours of contact with their mothers. The conclusion seemed to be that they had become familiar with their mothers' voices while they were in the womb.

The significance of learning before birth became apparent in another study, this time with guinea pigs. Two groups of pregnant guinea pigs were kept in separate rooms. One group heard the exaggerated sounds of a bantam hen clucking, while the other group heard no sound at all. The guinea pig mothers exposed to the sound of clucking were startled at first. They froze and their heart rates slowed – an automatic response by their bodies to help to reduce the risk of being detected by an unknown 'predator'. The bantam sounds were then played again and again, but each time the guinea pigs reacted less fearfully, until they ignored the sound altogether.

A little later, both groups of mothers gave birth and their babies were played the sound of the clucking hen. The group that had heard nothing while in the womb responded in the normal way – their heart rates slowed down and they remained as still as statues. The response of the youngsters born to the guinea pigs who had been exposed to the sound was less pronounced. They were familiar with the clucking sound and, like their mothers, had learned to ignore it.

LEARNING BY HABIT

The experiment showed that a baby can become accustomed to many sounds going on around its mother. At birth, therefore, it already has some experience of what is familiar and can be taken for granted, and what is frightening and should be ignored only at its peril.

HOW TO TAKE CYANIDE AND SURVIVE

Plants protect themselves from the ravages of herbivores by producing poisons. In the forests of Madagascar, for example, there is a type of bamboo that is highly toxic. The tips of its shoots contain cyanide in quantities that should deter even the most tolerant of vegetarians – about $1/500$ oz for every pound of bamboo (15 mg for every 100 g).

Yet there is one animal that eats it – the 27 lb (12 kg) golden bamboo lemur, one of three lemurs known to eat bamboo. The other two species, the grey gentle lemur and the greater bamboo lemur, feast on bamboo leaves and the thick bamboo trunks, leaving the poisonous shoots to the golden bamboo lemur.

It eats and digests about $17 1/2$ lb (500 g) of poisonous shoots per day – which is the equivalent of 12 times the lethal dose for humans. How it manages to do this is something of a mystery, although there are some possible explanations. One is that the lemur has learned, probably by some process of trial and error, that by eating the iron-rich soil in its home range it can neutralise the poison.

Ions in the soil combine with the cyanide to prevent the formation of the poison. Clay in the soil also acts much like kaolin in human medicine. It binds with substances in the gut to lessen their detrimental effects.

THRIVING ON POISON *The golden bamboo lemur can eat cyanide without ill effect. It is one of about 15 species of lemur living in Madagascar.*

Habituation is probably the simplest and most common form of learning. For instance, a pet cat will look up if you move your chair, but if you do so several times it will eventually get used to the creaking and not stir from its slumbers in front of the fire. Similarly, a snail placed on a table will retract into its shell if you tap the table. But if nothing untoward happens to it each time you tap, eventually it will become 'habituated' to the tapping and continue crawling on its way.

Habituation is, in fact, a negative learning process. An animal learns that something startling or potentially dangerous is

DANGER! *When danger threatens, a ringed-neck pheasant instinctively crouches in the undergrowth.*

of no consequence and can be ignored. If it reacted to every stimulus it received, it would be so edgy that it would never have time to feed, drink, sleep, find a home or

GROWING USED TO CHANGE

Marine worms living on the seashore are very sensitive to changes in light intensity, such as those caused by the shadow of a predator passing overhead. When exposed to repeated changes, however, the rate at which they grow used to them – or 'habituate' – varies. They habituate rapidly to sudden decreases in light but more slowly to moving shadows, even though the change in intensity is the same. Attack involves movement, and so the worms are more alert – and therefore less liable to habituate – with moving shadows.

reproduce, and it would die. Therefore nature has given it the ability to filter out all the unimportant sights, sounds, touches, vibrations and smells in order to concentrate on the ones that matter.

Chickens, turkeys and other members of the pheasant family instinctively crouch at the sight of an object moving overhead. It is part of a natural alarm and defence mechanism, a response to an approaching bird of prey. This automatic reaction, which the bird performs without ever having learned it, could be wasting valuable feeding time if it froze and crouched every time a flock of sparrows flew by or a leaf dropped, and so habituation or 'familiarisation' sorts out potentially dangerous flyers from harmless ones.

But how does a young bird know that a bird of prey is dangerous when it has never been attacked by one? The answer is that hawks, falcons and eagles are sufficiently rare for the bird to see them as a new shape each time. It therefore freezes and crouches automatically.

Animals that prey on others also become habituated. The common toad responds to anything that looks like food by turning its

FUSSY FEEDER *A common toad will only feed when confronted with live, edible prey.*

head towards the source before pushing out its sticky tongue to capture it. If, in an experiment, non-edible prey is presented continually from the same source, the toad will eventually learn to leave it alone. In the wild, this ability to ignore certain stimuli has survival value. If the toad tried to capture everything that looked like food, it would waste a huge amount of time. On the other hand, it cannot afford to ignore something that is good to eat. The habituation process offers a compromise between these different pressures.

Interestingly, habituation has been shown to occur in all animals, from the simplest single-celled creatures to the most complex, and there is some evidence to suggest that each living cell in the body can respond in the same way.

There is also positive learning, in which an animal learns about things and events that are useful to it. It is known scientifically as 'instrumental' learning, and it works by trial and error. A bird building its first nest, for instance, might incorporate all manner of strange things – strands of wire, shards of glass, scraps of paper, empty cans – before it learns that grass, twigs, lichens and moss are best for strength and insulation. From its own experience, it has discovered the benefits of using the right materials. It has modified its behaviour and has received a reward, in this case a properly functioning nest in which it can safely raise the next generation.

BY TRIAL AND BY ERROR

A tree-living animal must also learn by experience about its precarious tree-top home. In a Madagascar forest, a baby sifaka lemur clings on tightly to its mother, but eventually curiosity gets the better of it and it takes its first steps into the branches. It momentarily lets go of its mother's fur and is immediately confronted with a vertical drop of many yards through a tangle of branches to the ground below. But it does not hesitate, lured on by the irresistible need for independence that is common to all primates of its age. Under its mother's watchful eyes, it rehearses the movements that will eventually allow it to follow its parents in the daily quest for food.

HOME DELIGHTS *By trial and error a cliff swallow finds the best mud consistency for a cosy clay nest.*

Like most diurnal primates, it relies primarily on good eyesight. It experiments and makes mistakes, but it learns. It tests the resistance of branches, allows itself to fall short distances to improve its landing, and progressively increases the distance it jumps. Despite the number of different things it must learn, it quickly gets the hang of moving safely about its forest home. A wrong move or miscalculation of distance could cost the young lemur an eye or even its life.

After several months of trial and (hopefully not too much) error, the lemur is able to jump competently from tree to tree. It can walk along branches with the balance of a tightrope walker, and swing about nonchalantly suspended by hands or feet. It has come a long way from the delicate and clumsy baby that defied the laws of gravity all those months ago.

Young birds of prey need to master these laws, too. Not only must they learn to fly but also to catch prey. Falcons and hawks have a sensitive period between the third and seventh weeks of their lives when they have to be exposed to live prey in order to become efficient aerial hunters. At first, the young killers are reluctant to approach their intended victims. The prey's movements, which will later stimulate them to attack, frighten them. But gradually they overcome their fears and go in for practice kills. A goshawk does this even without its parent's example. It throws its legs forward to grasp the prey, but jumps backwards and then attacks again. Often during these first attacks it relinquishes the prey, which then flees. Eventually it learns the correct hold and is able to dispatch its prey with a bite

LEAVING HOME *A baby sifaka clings to its safe 'platform', not yet ready to explore a new world.*

to the neck. Later it will learn, by experience, to strangle or squeeze it to death in its powerful claws. The reward may be a squirrel, rabbit or grouse.

THE ART OF DISCRETION

Animals also have to learn what to avoid – whether disease, discomfort or danger. This form of learning is known as 'avoidance learning'. Florida scrub jays and other birds that like to catch and eat butterflies may get stomachache if they consume a brightly coloured monarch butterfly. The caterpillar feeds on milkweed plants, from which it extracts a foul-tasting poison. When it changes into a butterfly, it keeps the poison in its body. Its bright orange

STEER CLEAR! *The gaudy colours of monarch butterfly caterpillars (far left) and adults (left) inform birds that they are bad to eat.*

never seen such a thing before, the chicken was cautious and even showed signs of alarm. Eventually the bird, stimulated most probably by both curiosity and hunger, pecked at the mealworm and discovered that it was, after all, good to eat. It gobbled down all subsequent mealworms with gusto, having forgotten its original fear.

IMAGES OF PREY

The chicken remembers what mealworms look like so that it can spot them in the future and recognise that they are something worth eating. There is evidence that animals possess what are known as 'search images' to do this. Toads, for instance, will try to eat dangly pieces of moss if they have recently fed on spiders, and will attempt to eat long, thin *(continued on page 40)*

and black coloration is a warning to birds to leave it alone. But an inexperienced scrub jay has not learned to associate black and red stripes with a bad taste in the mouth. It must catch the butterfly, experience its foul flavour and regurgitate it before it learns that monarch butterflies are not good to eat.

Nevertheless, a balance has to be sought between caution and obtaining a meal. In one experiment, a domestic chicken was presented with a live mealworm. Having

PINE CONES AND THE MEMORY TEST

Memory is usually considered to be the ability to recall or perform some previously learned piece of information or behaviour. There are three types: immediate memory, in which information is retained for a few thousandths of a second; short-term memory, in which a limited amount of information may be stored for several minutes (long enough to look up a telephone number and dial it); and long-term memory, in which vital information is stored for long periods.

Some animals have remarkable memories. These include the hundreds of species of digger wasps around the world. In an experiment conducted by the Nobel prize-winner Niko Tinbergen, a circle of pine cones was placed

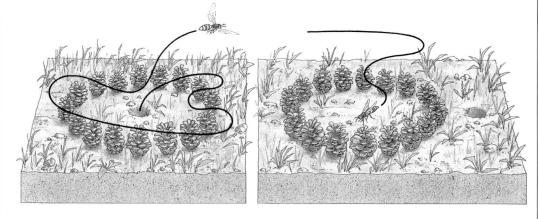

around the entrance hole to a female digger wasp's nest while she was still inside it.

When she emerged, the wasp flew around the immediate area, apparently checking out the position of the pine cones, and then flew off to forage. While she was away the experimenter moved the circle of

pine cones to one side, and on her return the wasp made a beeline for the relocated cones.

She had remembered the position of her nest entrance as being at the centre of the circle of cones. As a result, she was totally confused after the cones had been moved to a different place.

FINDING THE WAY *A digger wasp uses landmarks such as a circle of pine cones (above left) to find its way to and from the entrance to its nest. If the landmark cones are moved slightly, the digger wasp loses its bearings (above).*

THE SHAPE OF GOOD FOOD   *The peregrine learns and remembers that a pigeon-shaped bird is food.*

MIGRATING BIRDS

Birds are remarkable travellers. Some, like the Arctic tern, the short-tailed shearwater and the golden plover, fly from one end of the globe to the other and then back again all in a single year. Others, such as the North American pine grosbeak and blue grouse, restrict their travels to the slopes of a single mountain, moving from the top to the bottom to take advantage of seasonally favourable conditions. But whatever the distance and whatever the obstacles in their path – mountains, oceans and deserts

– birds must be able to find their way. They do this partly by instinct but more importantly by learning.

The urge to migrate is thought to be inherited. The maiden voyages of some small birds are also believed to be instinctive. The inexperienced birds are guided by inbuilt instructions that enable them to head off roughly in the right direction. European garden warblers, for example, are programmed to head south-west in August and September from the more northerly parts of the Continent to the

Iberian Peninsula. Instinct then instructs them to head south in October across the Straits of Gibraltar and on to west Africa, and then north again the following April to return to Europe. As they gain more experience and pick up navigational cues – the position of the Sun in the sky by day and star patterns at night – they can override their innate flight plans and put down at known refuelling stops, such as oases.

Some birds learn these cues before they leave. Gull and tern chicks have been seen sitting in their scrapes in the ground

at night and gazing at the heavens as they learn their star maps. In the Northern Hemisphere, they recognise that stars in the Pole Star cluster are in the same position in the sky because they are above the Earth's axis of rotation. No doubt, they observe the Sun's apparent movement across the sky by day and its angle of inclination. This information must be remembered for their future travels.

Fledged terns make reconnaissance sorties over the nest and surrounding area, searching for feeding and roosting sites, so

RECONNAISSANCE *Before heading south, birds often fly widely around their nest site, learning the locations of useful landmarks.*

that when they return from their sojourn in the Southern Hemisphere they will be able to recognise the landscape of the nesting site.

Young swans and geese most likely learn parts of their migration routes by following their parents. They normally fly in family parties, the youngsters memorising the positions of prominent landmarks such as lakes, rivers and mountains along the way. They are also capable of finding their way alone, as Canada geese sometimes do, indicating that innate instructions are available to them.

It is probable that birds, even experienced migrants, rely on both instinct and learning to find their way. They use a form of 'piloting' through familiar, remembered landmarks when setting out and when they arrive at their destinations, but depend on innate navigational instructions to cross featureless deserts and oceans.

A bird establishes its position and course by reference to the position of heavenly bodies in the sky. And, like its modern human counterpart, it has a back-up system that it can rely on in bad weather. This back-up is in effect an inbuilt compass, enabling the bird to exploit the lines of force in the Earth's geomagnetic field. Responding to the direction of these lines of force, it seems, are tiny particles of magnetite – a magnetically sensitive iron oxide – that are linked to nerves in the bird's nose region. With this navigational aid, the bird can identify its location, no matter where on the globe it happens to be at the time.

Birds often have more than one strategy for dealing with everyday tasks. Night-

flyers, for example, check their course during the darkness by plotting the position of the stars, but they set their original course at sunset. As the Sun dips below the western horizon, the plane of polarisation of light (roughly, the angle of the light waves' vibrations) runs directly north-south, so a spring migrant in the Northern Hemisphere can set its northerly course from this freely available information.

IMPRINTING *After it hatches, a snow goose gosling imprints on its parents, who will teach it about their migration route.*

LEARNING THE WAY *Huge flocks of snow geese stop off in Quebec. Many youngsters fly in family parties, learning migration routes from their parents.*

RETALIATION *A martial eagle preying on a baby gazelle finds itself under attack from the youngster's relatives.*

pushes them to investigate any new object in their environment, and if the object looks at all edible, they like to taste it. So, it came about that an inquisitive tit chanced upon a bottle of milk, attracted no doubt by its colourful top. The enterprising bird pierced the top with a series of hammer blows with its beak, the same method tits use to dislodge insect larvae from tree bark, and thus found a brand-new source of food. The discovery was not forgotten and after that the bird returned time and time again to repeat the exercise.

Other birds in the neighbourhood were equally curious and watched the pioneer. It is enough for one tit to see another enjoying some food for it to fly in for a slice of the action. Gradually the new trend caught on and the thefts spread from their centre of origin. The habit has provided an example of how learned behaviour is passed on among individuals in a population.

objects if they have just demolished a juicy earthworm. Similarly, the stomachs of some trout have been found to contain inanimate objects that closely resemble the food they have been eating. It seems that the prey leaves an image of itself in the mind of the animal.

This is particularly striking in small birds, such as great tits, that hunt well-camouflaged caterpillars. Some caterpillars look remarkably like twigs and, at first glance, are almost invisible. Even the birds are fooled – but not for long. It may take some time to find the first caterpillar, but once one is found the feast begins. The birds have acquired a search image and can recognise the caterpillars despite their cryptic shape and coloration.

MILK TAPPING

Having successfully caught, killed or collected some food – whether fish, meat or vegetable – a youngster must learn how to eat it.

Young great tits, for example, learn how to hold down a winter moth caterpillar with one or both feet while they tear at it with their bill. Young red squirrels are able to break open hazelnuts, but they are

rather clumsy at first. They gnaw at random and find the kernel more by luck than design. Gradually they learn that by biting through the long groove along one side they can push their teeth into the crack and split the nut in two. Some animals that live alongside people have put this learning ability to good use to come up with some remarkable pieces of behaviour.

During the 1930s, people living in some areas of England noticed when they went to collect the milk from the doorstep in the morning that someone had got there first. The bottles had already been opened and the layer of cream at the top had disappeared. It turned out that the thieves were none other than titmice – bluetits, coal tits and great tits.

These birds dedicate much of their day to looking for food, mostly consisting of caterpillars, grubs and worms. Their curiosity

NUTCRACKER *The red squirrel develops its own nut-cracking technique.*

In Japan, a troop of monkeys was even more inventive. The troop consisted of 20 or so Japanese macaques on the island of Koshima in southern Japan. They lived in

the wild, but while they were the subjects of a study of macaque behaviour, they were fed regularly with sweet potatoes.

In September 1953, about a year after the first potato meal, the attention of the scientists was drawn to an 18-month-old female they called Imo. She picked up a potato covered with sand and went to a nearby stream to wash it before eating. By October, a young male called Semucshi, who was Imo's playmate, had picked up the technique and he, too, was washing his food regularly.

Next to catch on in January 1954 was Imo's mother, Eba, and another macaque about the same age as Imo. In the following two years Imo's younger brother, elder sister, niece and four unrelated macaques took to washing their food before eating it. Interestingly, the cultural transmission was restricted to Imo's peer group. Of the older members of the troop, only Imo's mother and another adult took up the food-washing technique. They

PREY-FINDER *The great tit has an in-built 'search image' for caterpillars.*

MAKING MAPS IN THE MIND

When an animal has found a feeding site or resting place, it will probably want to find it again, possibly approaching from a different direction. For this it needs a map, not on paper but in its brain. Many animals possess such maps, but one has demonstrated notable cartographic skills: the honeybee. In tests, honeybees have been trained to use a particular path between their hive and a source of food. If removed from the hive and released from a place where they can see the hive but not the food, they are able to fly straight to the food without passing via the hive. They have learned and remembered the surrounding geography. They can then use novel routes, without deviating to a familiar site.

MIND MAP *A bee homes in on a flower. A 'mind map' enables it to find its way back to its hive, without retracing its path (below).*

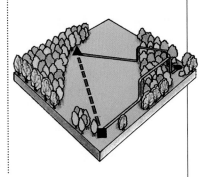

CREAMING OFF *British blue tits have learned to peck milk-bottle tops and sip the cream.*

performed it clumsily at first but slowly became more efficient.

By 1959, some seven years later, when the young washing macaques became mothers, the apprentices turned teachers and it was they who taught their young-sters by example. The breastfeeding babies watched what their mothers were doing at the water's edge and grabbed any potato scraps that had been dropped. Fast learners acquired the skill by the time they were a year old.

Soon 36 out of 46 macaques above two years of age were washing potatoes, some improving the flavour of the sweet pota-toes by dipping them in saltwater rather than freshwater. They would even bite the potatoes once or twice so that the salt penetrated them.

IMO'S INGENUITY

In the meantime, Imo surprised the scientists once more with another bout of gastronomic innovation. On this occasion, the macaques were given some wheat. It was simply thrown on the sand for them, and the troop found it incredibly difficult and time-consuming to separate wheat grains from sand grains.

Imo came to the rescue. She grabbed a handful of wheat and sand and threw it into a pool. The sand sank and the wheat floated. All she had to do was scoop it carefully from the surface. Again, it was the young macaques rather than the older animals who took up the tradition, although they took more than a year to learn it.

They were understandably confused and more than a little suspicious that they apparently had to discard their food before it was cleaned. The relationship between acquiring the food and separating it from the sand was a more complex one for them to grasp. After all, in potato washing they could hold on to their potato and be satisfied that no other macaque was likely to steal it.

Imo was of high rank in the troop and there is some evidence that her privileged position influenced the speed with which these unique pieces of behaviour were taken up by the other members. There was, however, one additional side effect of potato washing. Very young Japanese macaques ride with their mothers by hanging on to their undersides. Every time they bent over to wash a potato the babies were ducked in the pool. As they grew older these youngsters learned that the sea can be fun and they were often seen frolicking at the water's edge.

The study was an important milestone in the study of animal behaviour, for it demonstrated that this young macaque had worked out how to put two elements together in order to solve a problem. Imo had been inventive. She had taken food and water and learned how to use them in a way that modified the characteristics of both. It was a remarkable thing for a macaque to do.

LEARNING TO WASH *A Japanese macaque washes a sweet potato in the sea before eating it.*

INGENIOUS
MEANS

2

ANIMAL TOOLS *Finches in the Galápagos Islands use tools to prise out tasty larvae.*

TOOL-USING, ELABORATE WEAVING AND SOPHISTICATED CIVIL ENGINEERING: NONE OF THESE SKILLS IS THE EXCLUSIVE PROPERTY OF HUMANS — ALL OCCUR IN THE ANIMAL WORLD, EVEN AMONG RELATIVELY HUMBLE CREATURES SUCH AS INSECTS. ANIMALS OF VARIOUS KINDS HAVE WORKED OUT HOW TO USE ANVILS, PROBES, ANGLING LINES AND IMPROVISED TOILET TISSUE AND FLY-SWATTERS. TERMITES CREATE AUTOMATIC AIR-CONDITIONING SYSTEMS FOR THEIR NESTS, AND HONEYBEES PRODUCE LIGHTWEIGHT BUT STURDY BUILDING MATERIALS TO CONSTRUCT THEIR COMBS. THERE ARE ANIMALS THAT MANUFACTURE PAPER AND BUILD TENTS, LODGES AND DAMS. ANIMALS ALSO HAVE THEIR OWN NATURAL MEDICINES.

IN IT TOGETHER *Weaver ants cooperate to mend a leaf nest.*

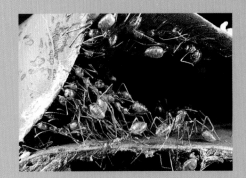

THE TOOLMAKERS

Tools are by no means exclusive to human beings. Naturalists now know that some other animals – birds and insects, as well as our nearest relatives, the chimpanzees – use and even manufacture tools.

Nearly 2 million years ago an animal that was part ape and part human made its first appearance on Earth. It walked upright and possessed a largish brain. More importantly, it had hands that were not only capable of grasping large objects, such as a tree branch, in a 'power grip', but could also pick up delicate things in a 'precision' pinch between finger and thumb.

The fossilised bones of the creature were found in rocks in Olduvai Gorge in Tanzania, and nearby broken animal bones and chopping instruments fashioned from round pieces of lava and quartzite were strewn around in so-called 'butchery sites'. The ape-man was given the scientific name *Homo habilis*, meaning 'handy man'. It was one of our earliest ancestors, a primitive version of ourselves (*Homo sapiens* – that is, 'wise man') and it manufactured a variety of simple stone tools, the predecessors of the vast array of sophisticated weapons and tools we have today. For a long time this toolmaking skill was one that many naturalists considered to be a purely human trait, setting us apart from other animals. Humankind alone was considered to be the sole maker and user of tools.

Then scientists made a remarkable discovery. They were watching chimpanzees and saw them 'fishing', not for fish with rod and line, but for termites with long stems of grass.

Once again, nature had surprised them with its resourcefulness. Today we now know of at least 18 species of monkeys and apes, several other species of mammals, many birds and even some insects that make and use tools.

TERMITE FISHING

Tools can be taken from the environment and used as they are, or they can be modified for a number of specific uses. As a kind of extension of the mouth, beak, claws or hand, they help animals to obtain food, to scare off predators, and even sometimes to take care of their own bodies. Chimpanzees, which share with human beings about 99 per cent of their genetic make-up, are the undisputed champions among them. They are humanity's nearest relatives, and certainly seem to be the 'cleverest' of the big apes.

For example, groups of chimpanzees in different parts of Africa 'fish' for honey, termites and ants, each group in its own particular way. At Gombe Stream National Park in Tanzania, 'honey fishing' is a relatively simple activity. An animal takes a thin, supple twig, pushes it inside a

DIGGING FOR DINNER *A wild Zambian chimpanzee uses a tool to dig for termites.*

NUTCRACKER *A Liberian chimpanzee learned partly from its mother and partly from experience how to crack nuts by using a tool.*

honeybee nest, retrieves it, and licks off the honey, like a child eating a lollipop.

Catching termites is slightly more difficult. First, a suitable twig must be found and fashioned, preferably from a pliable material with few snags, since termite tunnels tend not to be straight. Grasses, vines, bark, palm frondlets and twigs make good fishing rods, and the chimpanzees inspect many of them closely and carefully before selecting one. Any leaves are stripped off the stem and its diameter is modified by removing slithers of bark. During the wet season, when termites live at the surface of their nests, the twig is usually about 11 in (28 cm) long, but in the dry season, when the insects live deeper down, the chimps make the fishing rod a good deal longer, perhaps up to 5 ft (150 cm).

During its manufacture, the chimp pauses from time to time as if 'thinking' about the task in hand. When the tool is complete, it carries the twig or grass stem in its mouth. The termite nests are often as much as 109 yd (100 m) or so away and out of sight of the 'tool-making' site. The chimpanzee inspects several nests and then settles down beside one to start fishing. It pushes the twig into

a hole in the nest, vibrates it slightly and waits. After a few moments, enough soldier termites have 'attacked' the stick, clinging on with their powerful mandibles, for the chimp to withdraw the stick and pull its catch through its hand and then into its mouth or directly between its teeth.

During a termite-fishing session, the twig becomes frayed at the end or bent, so the chimp bites off the damaged sections. When the tool is too short, the chimp discards it and seeks out another. Some chimps will even climb high into a tree in search of a suitable vine, or venture far from the termite nest to find a twig. Several tools may be picked at the same time, the 'spares' tucked away in the groin or laid on the ground nearby. Young observers often accompany a fishing chimp, waiting for the 'tutor' to finish so they can try themselves. They pick up the adult's discarded twig and attempt to fish at the same termite hole.

Termite fishing seems to be universal among chimpanzees: similar behaviour is found in such different places as the Mahale Mountains in Tanzania and the Mount Asserik region of Senegal. Even chimps that had been removed from the wild in Guinea, kept in captivity as beach photographers' 'stooges' for several years, and then rehabilitated back into the wild on an island in the Gambia, showed that they had not lost the knack of fishing for termites. They had learned many years previously from adults in their wild troop and had remembered the technique.

The chimpanzees at Okorobiko, Mbini, in Equatorial Guinea, however, are less refined. They use much larger sticks to poke holes in the termite nests and then pick out the insects with their fingers.

HOW TO DIP FOR ANTS

'Ant dipping' requires similar tools, but it is more hazardous. The ants in question are driver ants, a nomadic species whose huge columns scour the countryside for any living thing. During the day the queen and her entourage bivouac, and it is these large gatherings that attract the chimps.

An ant-dipping 'wand' can be anything from 6 in (15 cm) to over a yard long. The shorter sticks catch fewer ants per dip and the dipper is in greater danger of being attacked. The technique is simple: the chimpanzee thrusts the stick into the nest and the ants stream up it. Watching their progress carefully, the dipping chimp waits

ANIMALS THAT TAKE MEDICINES

Sick animals take medicines just as humans do. In the early morning, chimpanzees in East Africa may walk for 20 minutes or more in search of aspilia plants, members of the sunflower family. They collect the leaves and massage them in the mouth for about 15 seconds, without chewing. They wrinkle their noses, like children taking a foul-tasting medicine, and swallow the leaves whole. Aspilia leaves are rich in a red oil called thiarubrine-A, a potent drug that kills parasitic worms, bacteria

and fungi. Similarly, chimpanzees eat plants of the vernonia (bitter leaf) family. An ailing chimp with a stomach disorder will chew vernonia shoots and suck up the bitter juice. The plant has antibacterial properties and boosts the immune system against viruses.

In North America, grizzly bears and black bears chew on *Ligusticum porteri*, a plant in the lovage family. They swallow the masticated roots to treat worms and bacterial infections or spit them into their

coats, where they massage the juice into the fur to kill parasites such as ticks and fungi.

In South America, female howler monkeys eat some as yet unidentified plants directly before or after copulation and at no other time. Speculation has it that by eating the plants the mothers predetermine the sex of their offspring – mothers prefer to have more male offspring to offset the odds that males are likelier to be killed than females.

until the leading ants are just about to reach its hand. It then withdraws the stick, and using its other hand, sweeps the ants into a writhing mass and pops them into its mouth. A competent dipper can scoop up more than 300 ants in one dip.

Chimps also use sticks to enlarge the entrance to a hornbill's nest. The female bird and her fledglings are holed up inside, the male regularly supplying them with food. They make the opening to the nest as small as possible and partly seal it with a mixture of saliva and clay. The chimps use the stick to break through the hard clay, so that they can reach inside for the fledglings. In much the same way, they winkle grubs out of rotting wood, break into the hard, football-sized nests of tree ants, and pillage underground bees' nests.

HAMMER-AND-ANVIL TECHNOLOGY

In West Africa, chimpanzees use large, stout sticks and rocks to crack open nuts, commonly coula and panda nuts, with very hard shells. To get at the nutritious kernels inside, the chimps learn a hammer-and-anvil technique, a rock or tree root serving as the anvil and a stone or branch as the hammer. Stones, though, are rare on the forest floor and sometimes have to be carried several hundred yards to the food. The chimps may break a large stone in two, but usually they choose the right tool such as a piece of hard granite.

Great precision is needed. Nuts are so hard that only a pressure of 3530 lb (1600 kg) can break the shell, but if the chimps bring down the stone with too much force both shell and kernel are squashed. So, they proceed with care. First, they crack the shell with powerful blows and then, with more gentle ones, they release the kernel without crushing it, repositioning

FOR FOOD AND DEFENCE
Chimpanzees use tools for obtaining food and water, and for defence. Here they 'fish' for termites, use twigs to scoop up water and beat off a roving leopard with sticks.

POWERS OF CONCENTRATION — PEANUTS AND MONKEYS

The ability of South American capuchin monkeys to use tools has been studied in recent years by the Italian primate expert Elisabetta Visalberghi. She was struck by the similarity between their behaviour and chimpanzees', especially an apparent ability to form a mental picture of a problem that needs solving.

In an experiment, some capuchins in captivity were presented with a Plexiglas tube about 12 in (30 cm) long containing a peanut. They were given sticks, some too wide to push into the tube, and others with projections that needed removing. They were then left with the puzzle of how to get at the peanut. They split the sticks and removed any leaves, one individual solving the problem in under 30 minutes, although two hours was more usual. One enterprising female forsook the sticks altogether and blew out the peanut. But feats like these were the exception rather than the rule, and the fact that a capuchin succeeded once did not ensure its success the next time. Neither did the least skilful improve their success by watching their more crafty companions. In effect, the capuchins were capable of solving complex problems, but not because they had a mental image of the tool's characteristics or because they understood what they needed to accomplish. They simply tried every possible way of tackling the problem.

GET THE PEANUT *In an experiment, South American capuchin monkeys were given Plexiglas tubes, each with a peanut stuck in it.*

They showed that they did not have the intellectual qualities possessed by the chimpanzee.

---

the nut continuously to make best use of the hammer and anvil.

On the Ivory Coast, one group of chimpanzees in the Tai National Park busies itself with nutcracking for about $2^1/2$ hours each day. Youngsters dangle from their mothers, watching carefully until the time comes for them to try for themselves. The technique is learned and passed down the generations from mother to infant – an example of cultural transmission.

SPONGING UP A DRINK

Having eaten their fill, chimpanzees may need something to wash it down, and here again they may use a tool to help them. Usually, a chimp will bend down and slurp up water with its mouth, but if the water is difficult to reach – for example, rainwater trapped inside a hollow tree trunk – it uses a 'sponge' to soak up the water. The sponge consists of crumpled leaves that have been chewed to increase their absorbency. The leaves are dipped into the hollow and the liquid sucked from the 'sponge', the process repeated until the water is gone or the chimpanzee has quenched its thirst. Some individuals even use their leaf

sponges to drink from streams. Chimpanzees also use leaves as we would use tissues, wiping sticky fruit from face and hands, faeces from the bottom and semen from the penis. One individual was seen to

FUN AND TOYS FOR CHIMPS

Chimpanzees have 'toys'. These include strips of skin and hair from a kill that they drape over their shoulders, and stones and fruits that they bounce on the ground or toss from one hand to another. They also roll large round objects, such as strychnos fruits, on the ground. One chimpanzee was seen to throw a fruit high into the air and then catch it, a performance he then failed to repeat despite many tries. Chimpanzees use short sticks for tickling, an activity that can last for ten minutes, accompanied by boisterous laughing.

use a dead leaf to scrape out the last traces of fruit from the inside of a strychnos nut. Another used leaves to clean the inside of a baboon skull after a feast, and another chimpanzee used a bunch of leaves to brush aside bees from the surface of their nest before stealing their honey.

Like humans, chimpanzees and several other primates have discovered the value of tools as weapons. Confronted with a leopard, a group of chimps will seize sticks and stones, first brandishing them in defiance and then throwing them as missiles. Groups living on the savannah seem to have a better aim than those living in the forest.

Howler and spider monkeys living in the tropical forests of South and Central America also use weapons. They throw or drop sticks from the trees, shaking the branches in an intimidating way. A wary predator will probably make a rapid retreat. Capuchin monkeys have even been seen to drop sticks on ground-dwelling coatis (racoon-like animals), even though they were peacefully exploring the undergrowth below and posed no real threat.

Brown capuchins in the La Macarena National Park in Colombia are particularly adept at using tools and, like chimpanzees, have several ingenious ways of getting a meal. Local palm nuts gradually ripen, and when the juice inside becomes sweet and sticky with the consistency of thick yoghurt, these New World monkeys bite a hole with their long canine teeth and drink the juice. When the flow stops, they find a gruadua bamboo and strike the husk against it, shaking the last drops of the sticky juice down like a diner shaking and banging a ketchup bottle. In the ripe nut, the juice hardens and the monkeys use the bamboo as an anvil against which to crack the nut and extract it.

What all these primates have done is to use their ingenuity to increase their chances of survival. Each occupies what is known as a 'biotope'. This is a region marked out from other regions by certain physical conditions (such as temperature and rainfall) and biological conditions (such as the quality and quantity of food available, competition from its own kind, and problems from predators). Each

biotope is populated by a particular plant and animal community. As a part of that community, an animal is confronted by the challenges that its biotope presents, and it must find solutions in order to stay alive and reproduce.

Evolution accumulates these solutions. The weak, lacking the ingenuity to find an answer, succumb, and the fit, adapted to find and exploit novel solutions, survive. The mechanism works at two levels. First, chance plays a fundamental role since at the moment of birth all the genetic information contributed by an animal's parents combine. But an animal given the basic capacity to adapt – say, one conferred with some degree of 'intelligence' and the

ability to make use of tools – responds best to problems set by its environment.

At this level, selection proper intervenes. Environmental changes are continuous, and animals respond accordingly. Each species shows various ways of behaving aimed at keeping up with environmental change. Anatomical or physiological adaptations may be enough; otherwise, animals have to resort to more complex behaviour. It may be the simple piling up of materials to build a shelter or

CLAM-CRACKING *A Californian sea otter floats on its back and cracks a clam on a stone 'anvil' placed on its stomach.*

an animal may take more drastic or subtle action, like the use of tools. The super-intelligent primates are by no means the only animals to find this solution to their environmental challenges.

AN OTTER'S FAVOURITE MEAL

In the northern Pacific, the sea otter has joined that exclusive club. As their name suggests, sea otters spend most of their lives at sea – eating and breeding there. Their diet is varied – crabs, mussels, limpets, abalone, clams, fish, octopus and the occasional sea cucumber – although a local abundance of food will cause an individual otter to focus on one particular type.

Abalone is a favourite, but this large, limpet-like shellfish clings tenaciously to rocks and is difficult to remove. In order to do so, the otter finds a suitable stone and hammers at the shell, occasionally rising to the surface to breathe and then plunging back down and hammering energetically until the mollusc is dislodged. The otter then takes the shell to the surface and devours its contents eagerly. During the meal, it anchors itself by a frond of giant kelp to stop it drifting away, and floats on its back on the surface of the sea.

Bivalves – that is, shellfish with the two halves of their shell pulled tightly together – require a different technique. To break open these shells, the sea otter searches not for a rounded hammer but for a flat stone to serve as an anvil. It dives down, grabs a suitable stone about 4 in (10 cm) in diameter, and tucks it under its arm. It then pulls a clam or mussel free and swims back to the surface. Floating on its back, it places the anvil on its stomach, takes the

HOW TO CRACK AN EGG
A banded mongoose throws an egg between its hind legs in order to smash it on the ground or rocks behind.

shellfish in its forepaws and strikes it repeatedly against the stone until the shell cracks open. Not wishing to discard the anvil, the otter tucks the stone under its arm and plunges below to find another shell.

SNAILS, CRABS AND EGGS

The marsh mongoose of Africa has a similar problem with crabs and snails that it, too, solves with the help of an anvil or piece of rocky ground. It takes the prey in its forepaws, stands erect on its hind legs, and then flings it to the ground repeatedly until the carapace cracks.

The Egyptian mongoose, has a passion for eggs but has difficulty cracking large ones with its teeth because its gape is too small. Instead, it stands in front of a large rock, takes the egg in its paws, stands on its hind legs and throws the egg with its forelegs until it smashes against the rock. In Madagascar, the ten-striped mongoose goes one better. It lies on its back near a flat stone and, with its paws close together, throws an egg up into the air, whereupon the egg lands on the stone and cracks open.

Eggs are a particularly nutritious food and an ostrich egg is a single-course meal. Many savannah animals take advantage of such a bonanza – if they can avoid the wrath of the parent bird – but not all can cope with the tough shell.

Where size and strength are lacking, guile is an effective

MEAL FOR A VULTURE
Chance plays a big part as an Egyptian vulture tries to crack an ostrich egg by throwing stones at it.

substitute, and the shy Egyptian vulture has it. It breaks into the egg using a stone. It searches the ground for a suitable rock, then takes it in its bill and dashes it against the egg, until a crack appears and the bird can lever away pieces of eggshell. How the vulture learned to use stone tools is unknown, although young vultures have a tendency to throw objects such as small eggs in order to break them open. The ostrich egg is too large to throw but is recognisable as an egg. The hungry vulture, used to throwing small eggs, may have started to throw egg-shaped stones at the shell until it broke. The fact that other opportunistic birds have not picked up the habit suggests that vultures have the extra dexterity needed to do it successfully.

Other birds, however, have developed other tool-using skills. On the islands of the Galápagos Archipelago in the eastern Pacific lives a finch that has filled the niche normally occupied by woodpeckers. Not surprisingly, it has been named the 'woodpecker finch'. But it does not have the woodpecker's muscular neck, protruding tongue and chisel-like bill with which to lever off bark and wrinkle out burrowing beetle larvae. Instead, it uses a cactus spine or thin twig to do the same job.

DIGGER WASPS – HOW A MOTHER PROVIDES FOR HER YOUNG

Testing the fit
The mother holds the 'coping' stone in her mandibles as she tests its fit.

Coping stone
The stone protects the young wasp and its live food from scavengers and other predators.

Food supply
A paralysed caterpillar will provide fresh food for the wasp larva when it emerges from the egg.

Some individuals are more adept than others, and may even modify their selected spines. Some woodpecker finches retain their chosen implement between meals.

In much the same way, the orange-winged sittellas of Australia insert twigs into cavities containing insect larvae. They hold the tool first in the beak and then by the feet while they consume the morsel. In Tanzania, grey flycatchers have been seen fishing for termites using grass stems in the manner of chimpanzees.

The American brown-headed nuthatch is another bird that uses tools to compensate for physical limitations. It uses bark scales to lever other pieces of bark off tree trunks to get at the insect larvae hiding beneath. Similarly, the Australian white-winged chough has been seen to break into

PECKING WOOD *The Galápagos woodpecker finch prises out grubs using a cactus spine.*

SEALED IN *A mother digger wasp uses a small stone to seal the larva, along with a supply of food, into its burrow.*

freshwater mussels using part of the open shell of another mussel as a hammer and lever.

The green heron is an astute angler, and catches fish with an artificial lure. It breaks off small twigs and throws them onto the water in such a way that they resemble insects in distress. Any fish that comes to investigate becomes a meal itself. The heron strikes fast and grabs the fish before it can return to hiding. Some individuals use feathers instead of sticks – like human fly-fishers.

Among the insects themselves there are a few known tool-users. Solitary digger wasps excavate nest burrows for their larvae, which they provision with paralysed

prey. During the construction of the nest, the mother wasp holds a small stone in her mandibles and pats down the earth to compress it into a compact plug. In one species, the mother plugs her nest's entrance with a small pebble. Some observers see this as learned behaviour, but a more likely explanation is that it is an extension of the digging, filling and head-pounding process that is thought to be instinctive.

Perhaps the most remarkable of insect tool-users is the 'angling' assassin bug of Costa Rica. The tiny nymph of this species has a penchant for termites and has discovered a way of getting past the normally aggressive termite soldiers so that it can prey upon tasty workers without coming to any harm. First, the nymph 'dresses up'. It places small pieces of the termite nest on its body, which gives it the scent of the colony. Thus disguised, it sidles up to a nest entrance and grabs the next termite to emerge, injecting digestive enzymes into it and sucking it dry. It then uses the dried-out shell as a lure to catch more termites. Since nothing is wasted in a colony – certainly not the protein-rich skin of a dead termite – the undertakers come to remove the corpse and they, too, are grabbed. A bug has been seen to 'angle' in this way for up to three hours, consuming 30 termites – that is, one every six minutes.

NATURE'S ARCHITECTS

Insects were architects and engineers, birds were fine weavers, and beavers were dam-builders long before humans made their first crude mud huts or straw baskets, or blocked a river for the first time.

Early, man-like creatures that made and used the first stone tools were also the first home-builders. In Tanzania's Olduvai Gorge, stone circles have been found in rocks that also contain the fossilised bones and tools of early man. The circles may have been the bases of round, tent-like dwellings that were made of branches, grasses and leaves. The large stones probably served as anchors for the base of each shelter.

At the same time, bone refuse and discarded tools littered the ground just outside the circles, the quantity of debris indicating that a permanent or semi-permanent campsite had been established there. Such a settlement would only have worked if the individuals living there cooperated and communicated. It was the beginning of an order that eventually gave rise to enormous cities containing large and complex buildings whose construction required detailed planning and considerable forethought.

Animals do without all the fuss. They build their extraordinary structures – shelters, nests and 'advertisement' signs – following the instructions that are contained in their genes. Even the most capable of animal architects appears to work entirely from an innate blueprint . . . or does it?

At first sight, it is hard to imagine an insect or bird 'thinking' about design, fabric or form, but there are traces of such

SAFETY IN NUMBERS *Cape weavers build their nests close to each other for greater safety.*

MASKED WEAVER

BAYA WEAVER

GROSBEAK WEAVER

GREY-HEADED SOCIABLE WEAVER

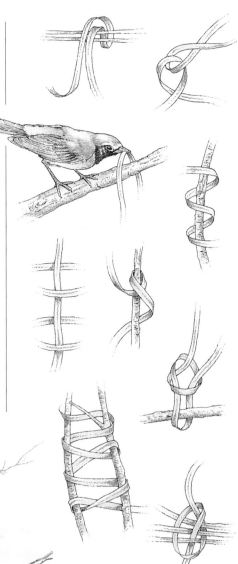

higher mental activities in the design and construction of some of their remarkable building works – in the nests of weaver-birds, for example.

The male weavers of Asia and Africa live up to their name by constructing nests of woven plant material in much the same way that human weavers make baskets or weave cloth. The raw materials must be flexible and strong, and may include strips torn from broad leaves, such as palm fronds, or long ribbon-like leaves of grasses or reeds.

Having selected a suitable hanging site – usually the thinner, outer branches of a tree that predators such as snakes cannot reach – the bird twists its first strip around a hanging twig or a pair of forked or parallel twigs. It does so by tying a knot: it holds the strip with one foot while using its beak to pass it behind and around the twig and through one of the loops. It pulls the simple half-hitch tight – but not too tight, for it might want to undo the knot at a later stage. Strips are then added to form a hanging ring onto which the rest of the nest is constructed. It is broadened by weaving strips together to form a brood chamber on one side, an antechamber on the other and a flight entrance below.

The weaving is done by interlacing lengthwise strips or 'warps' with crosswise strips or 'wefts', as in cloth and basket weaving. The strips, however, are shorter than the yarn used by a human weaver and so the bird has to secure the ends

repeatedly, either by tucking them into the mesh of the existing fabric or by tying them onto it with a knot. For this, the bird uses its beak to tie the knot while its feet hold down the nest's fabric.

The shapes of the nests vary from species to species: the masked weaver of East Africa constructs a simple globe, while Cassin's weaver hangs a 2 ft (60 cm) long entrance tube underneath its nest. But whatever the size and shape, the male bird must then put it on the market. He flaps his wings to advertise for a mate. If no females are forthcoming, the male must be prepared for more hard work. Females only occupy fresh, green nests. As soon as the sun takes its toll and the nest fabric turns brown, the weaverbird unpicks the weave, unties the knots, lets the old nest fall to the ground and starts all over again.

An inexperienced male weaverbird often makes a mess of nest building, his first attempts unravelling on the branch or

NEST WEAVE *Weaverbirds use complex knots (above) to build elaborate nests, such as that of the sociable weaver (left).*

falling off in the wind. Experience teaches him how the weave should run, how tightly the knots should be drawn, and which materials make the best nests, and he gradually perfects the technique. Although the instinctive plan is lodged in his brain, he must still learn how to construct the perfect nest.

Some species, such as the sociable weaver, build communal nests in trees. These are huge multistorey colonies. Up to 20 or 30 pairs may join forces, using twigs and strong savannah grasses to construct a massive structure 16½ft (5 m) in diameter. Each pair has its own nest within the fortress, and the many eyes and ears available watch and listen out for predators. The only major danger is when the colony grows too big for the branches on which it is perched and the entire edifice crashes to the ground.

COMMUNAL HOMES

The most sophisticated co-operative buildings, however, belong to the insects, especially the social insects such as ants, wasps, bees and termites. Of these, the termites – which look rather like white ants, but are in fact a kind of communal cock-

NEST AND ROOF *West African termites build nests with roofs to protect them against rain.*

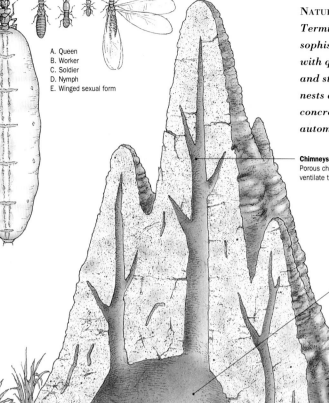

A. Queen
B. Worker
C. Soldier
D. Nymph
E. Winged sexual form

NATURE'S OFFICE BLOCK *Termites have highly sophisticated social structures, with queens, workers, soldiers and sterile nymphs. Their nests are rather like a modern concrete office building, with automatic air conditioning.*

Chimneys
Porous chimneys help to ventilate the mound.

Upper air space
Warm air from fermentation and the activity of the termites rises into an upper air space.

Air ducts
Warm air inside the nest cools down in a network of ducts in porous outer ridges or buttresses. Carbon dioxide diffuses out and oxygen enters.

Fungus chamber
Termites cultivate fungus as food. At the same time, the fermentation process warms the air.

Royal cell
The queen and her consort are incarcerated for life in a cell where they concentrate on the business of laying and fertilising eggs.

Foundations
Conical foundations support the main part of the nest.

Cellar
Cool air is drawn up from the cellar to fill the vacuum left by warm air rising through the nest.

roach – are undoubtedly the champion builders. Construction is undertaken by worker castes while the queen is busy laying eggs. Her consort fertilises them; winged males embark on seasonal nuptial flights, and soldiers guard the nest. Some species build nests in trees, others underground. The most remarkable by far, though, are the towering castles of clay that stand up to about 23 ft (7 m) high on the African grasslands – equivalent in human terms to a skyscraper 1 mile

---

COSY HOMES — PRIMATES WITH NESTS

Birds are not the only creatures that build nests. Many primates tuck into a cosy nest at night, and some even have daytime sleeping platforms. Dwarf bush babies and mouse lemurs build spherical nests of leaves; ruffed lemurs line nests of leaves with their own fur; gorillas have nests of crudely arranged vegetation on the ground; and orang-utans and chimpanzees bend and interlace branches and leaves to construct treetop sleeping platforms.

Construction improves with age, a young ape learning from its mother, with whom it sleeps until it is three or four years of age. The basic circular pattern of the chimpanzee nest is inherited, but the construction is refined by experience. Some individuals have even demonstrated how the first human shelters may have been made. Naturalists have found a single chimp nest, a gorilla nest and several nests made by orang-utans that actually have roofs.

Other apes have shown how a simple shelter may have evolved into a home. A chimpanzee with a bad cold will go to bed early – at 4 to 4.30 – and stay in bed till late in the morning. A couple of sufferers even constructed elaborate day-nest platforms and retired until they were feeling better. A pregnant orang-utan built a day nest in which she gave birth. It is not hard to imagine early hominids building nests for those in need, such as females ready to give birth. The move into family home life may have been a natural progression.

NESTLING DOWN *A young orang-utan builds a mat of twigs where it will spend the night.*

(1.6 km) high. Such a colony may contain more than 10 million individuals.

The first chambers of a 'termitarium' are started underground. A colony may already be of considerable size before the structure begins to rise above the savannah floor. It is made of earth mixed with saliva, the cement hardening like rock to form a fortress with walls about 20 in (50 cm) thick – impenetrable to all but a few spe-cialised termite-eaters, such as aardvarks and anteaters. The heat and carbon dioxide produced and trapped inside the nest by millions of busy, living bodies reach very high levels and would be dangerous to inhabitants if the termites had not come up with a fully automated, underground air-conditioning system.

The system works by convection. Heat and carbon dioxide rise, generated by the termites themselves and from fungus gardens they tend in chambers in the centre of the mound. In the fungus combs the temperature is 29.7°C (85.5°F), rising to 30°C (86°F) in the brood chambers above. The warm air accumulates in the attic, where the temperature drops slightly to 29.3°C (84.7°F), and is then forced into fine channels that run down ridges in the surface of the mound, close to the outside wall. Carbon dioxide diffuses out through the thin ridge walls; oxygen diffuses in, and the air is cooled to 25.5°C (77.9°F). The colder air drops into the cavernous cellar where it is humidified by a reservoir of ground water, and then drawn back up to the living area to fill the vacuum left by the rising warm air.

It is hard to believe that this ingenious system is the result solely of innate instructions passed from one generation to the next. Yet the termites do not learn how to build functional mounds: they do it automatically, each individual playing its small part for the good of the entire colony. The colony is more like a 'super-organism' – its individuals forming a

TOTTERING TOWERS *Termites' nests rise from the grasslands of South Africa's Transvaal.*

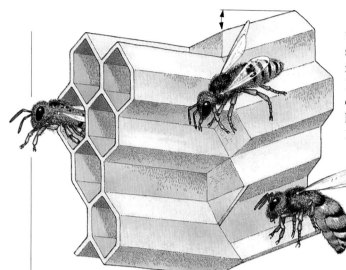

BEES AS ENGINEERS *Honeybees build combs with the cells tilted upwards, to stop the honey running out.*

CHECK UP *A honeybee uses the tips of its antennae to check the thickness of a cell wall and measure its elasticity*

BUILT TO BUILD *The bee itself is a remarkable example of nature's engineering.*

cooperative unit to propagate their genes – and it has been honed by millions of years of evolution to create the sophisticated society we see today.

BUSY AS A BEEHIVE

The African honeybee is the most studied social insect of all and it, too, is capable of building complex structures, not of clay but of wax combs in hollow trees or rock crevices. The combs hang vertically and have cells on both sides separated by a wall down the middle. The walls of the cells form regular hexagonal prisms – a shape that utilises all the available space without any wastage. A full honeycomb measuring $14^1/2 \times 9$ in (37×23 cm) might contain up to 4 lb (1.8 kg) of honey, yet the wax weighs just $1^1/2$ oz (42.5 g).

To start a comb, the worker bees line up and then form tight building clusters. At the centre of each ball of bees, the temperature is maintained at 35°C (95°F), the warmth needed to produce and manipulate wax. The wax is secreted from glands underneath a bee's abdomen. It appears as flakes picked up by the bee's hind legs and transferred to the forelegs and mandibles; it is then passed to 'chewers' who knead and mix the secretion thoroughly with saliva.

Construction begins at the top, with building clusters starting at several sites along the ceiling of the nest. The first parts of the comb taper downwards; the side walls of the first cells are made while adjoining cells are being started lower down. Gradually, the hexagonal cells coalesce, from the top downwards, with no visible joins and with cell walls meeting at exactly 120° – a skilful operation considering that the workers are constantly changing and no individual stays to finish a complete cell. Somehow, each new recruit understands what stage the construction has reached.

The cells jut out from the back wall at an angle of 13°, just enough to prevent the honey from running out. Brood cells differ slightly in size and shape depending on the inmate. The cells for worker larvae are $1/5$ in (5 mm) from wall to wall, while those for drones are $6/25$ in (6.2 mm); the thickness of the walls is $3/1000$ in (0.073 mm) for worker cells and $4/1000$ in (0.092 mm) for drone cells. The precision of these builders is astounding, and to achieve it they quite literally use their heads.

The worker bee's head hangs at a particular angle to the vertical, and its position is monitored by a tactile organ of sensory bristles that gives her accurate information about the angles of the walls. The size of the cells is measured by the tips of her front legs, and the thickness of the walls is determined by the tips of the antennae.

Wax is not the only construction material used by honeybees. They also collect plant resins for filling in gaps or holes. In the autumn, when draughts from cracks begin to make life uncomfortable, foraging workers collect resin, gnawing it from the sticky buds on trees. It also has a defensive use. If a small creature invades the nest it is killed and then covered with resin to mummify it and to prevent it from decomposing and spoiling the nest site.

Resin is also mixed with the wax, either to make it go further or to alter the melting temperature. In southern Italy, for example, where the outside temperature

FIELD NEST *A harvest mouse anchors its high-level nest near the tops of grass stems.*

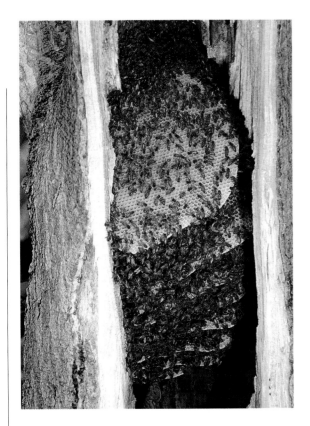

SWEET AS HONEY *Bees swarm over a comb built in an ailanthus tree of tropical Asia.*

can soar during the summer and melt the wax combs, resin raises the point at which the wax starts to melt and saves the colony. In other parts of Italy, the resin collected by bees, which is known as propolis, was one of the secret ingredients in the lacquers used by the great violin makers.

INSECT BRAIN POWER

To achieve all this, insects have a control centre. Like most animals they have a brain, and the more highly developed species have a brain of greater complexity than primitive ones. The honeybee and some other social insects (but not the termite) are at the zenith of insect brain development, with a large *corpora pedunculata* or 'mushroom body'. This is the part of the brain responsible for coordinating information from the sense organs and deciding on any action to be taken. It serves, it is thought, the higher mental functions – especially establishing associations. Scientists have suggested that its development in bees, wasps and ants is connected with the ability of these insects to learn.

Learning – whether by example or experience – has been firmly established in the higher vertebrates such as birds and mammals, and birds and mammals both include artisans amongst their ranks.

But mammals' constructions, bar a few exceptions, come nowhere near the complexity of the building work of birds. Arctic polar bears, for instance, dig ice dens that are scarcely more than hollows in compacted snow. The rat-like bandicoot of Australia is a little more sophisticated, scraping leaves and other ground litter together to create a breeding chamber. The Chilean marsupial – the *monito del monte*, or colocolo – builds spherical nests out of water-repellent bamboo leaves among fallen logs or tree roots.

The common ringtail possum of Australia constructs a spherical nest of grass and bark. The European dormouse builds a globular nest, lined with hairs and feathers, in a hole in a tree or the crook of a branch, and the harvest mouse weaves a nest of straw. Golden-rumped elephant shrews in the African forests gather together several piles of leaves, 3 ft (1 m) wide, in which they hide from predators, and North American pack rats create mounds of sticks and other debris in front of their burrows.

MUSKRAT RAMBLES

But the real engineers of the mammal world are the lodge builders of the north: muskrats and beavers. Muskrats – large rat-like rodents resembling small beavers but really related to voles – live in the colder northern lands of Europe, Asia and North America, where they construct their homes in large, shallow lakes with plenty of plant life in water up to 3 ft (1 m) deep. They mostly choose to build amongst waterside weeds, although they also dig burrows, particularly when they live on the seashore or close to rivers where a lodge of sticks would be quickly broken up.

ARCTIC SHELTERS *Polar bears dig winter ice dens and rest in snow holes such as these.*

With the approach of winter, they repair their relatively simple dwellings or build new ones, where they will spend the cold, dark months. The lodge itself is constructed in shallow water over a mound of mud. Pondweed, horsetail stalks and other plant material is heaped on to the mound until the dome-shaped lodge rises up to 3 ft (1 m) above the surface of the water. The muskrat burrows into the mud and vegetation, creating several escape holes and a hollowed-out living space in which it can sit out the winter weather.

Beavers are even more impressive builders. They often live in inhospitable places in northern latitudes where a warm, dry home is essential if they are going to survive the harsh winter conditions. The dwelling must be sufficiently large for an entire family of 12-15 individuals to live comfortably throughout the winter months, and it must be safe from the predatory attentions of hungry coyotes, wolves and lynxes. The beavers' answer to the problem is to build a grand lodge, which, as for a medieval castle, they surround with a deep moat. They maintain the level of

THIEVING BOWERBIRDS GO COURTING

Bowerbirds from Australia and New Guinea use twigs and leaves to build structures known as 'bowers'. These are not nests but advertisements that demonstrate the prowess of the builders – courting male bowerbirds. Each species builds a different structure, ranging from leaf-strewn stages to maypoles and large tents. But all adorn them with paraphernalia that includes colourful parrot feathers, snail shells, leaves, flower petals and human refuse, such as brightly coloured pieces of plastic and spent shotgun cartridges.

The bowers and their decorations are considered 'secondary sexual characteristics', like the peacock's ostentatious tail or the plumes of a bird of paradise. The bower is a display area for the sometimes brilliantly coloured males, where, to attract females, they flare their plumage, prance in postures of begging or aggression, and emit a variety of calls. The drab females judge a male's suitability by the quality and exuberance of his display and of his bower – an indication of his fitness as a father. They visit several bowers and choose the best mates.

The male satin bowerbird collects mainly blue objects, scattering them in front of his 'avenue' bower, built of two parallel walls of twigs, in order to impress a mate. Blue objects are therefore at a premium in satin bowerbird society and pilfering is rife. Some males not only steal from their neighbours, they destroy their bowers as well. Those that retain both their bowers and ornaments are those that dominate other males.

SHOWING OFF *A male satin bowerbird displays his handiwork to a female (below). The bowers include towers, tents and maypoles (right).*

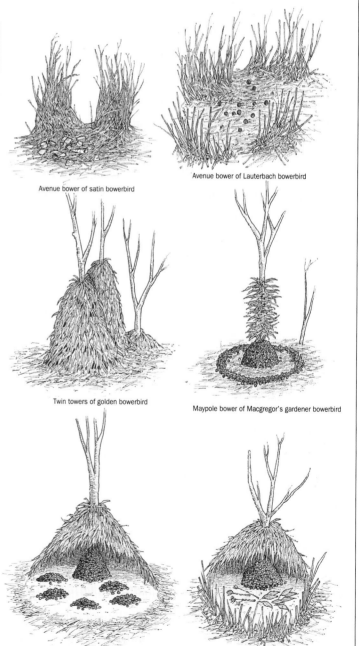

Avenue bower of satin bowerbird

Avenue bower of Lauterbach bowerbird

Twin towers of golden bowerbird

Maypole bower of Macgregor's gardener bowerbird

Tent-like bower of Vogelkop gardener bowerbird

Tent-like bower of orange-crested gardener bowerbird

TEETH FOR TIMBER
*A beaver's front teeth
are designed for gnawing.*

BUSY AS A BEAVER *Beavers
fell every aspen tree in the
vicinity in order to build their
enormous dams.*

water in the moat artificially with the help of another huge construction, the beaver dam. The choice of building site is critical.

A new pair of beavers looking to set up home will identify a small valley with a stream running through it as a suitable building site. They build the dam first, mainly of timber and mud. The beavers use their chisel-like front teeth to gnaw through the wood and fell the trees in surrounding forests. They favour saplings and small trees with a girth less than 1 ft (30 cm), and chop them into $1^{1}/_{2}$ to 8 ft (0.5 to 2.5 m) lengths. They remove the bark for food, and haul the logs to the riverside, where construction begins.

First, they push the stout branches vertically into the stream bed, with thinner saplings, twigs and leaves placed across them. Large rocks are carried into the stream, and their weight used to help anchor the entire structure. Mud and gravel from the stream bed are added to cement the vegetation together. The upstream side of the dam is built almost vertically and is covered with mud to make it watertight; the other side, up to $6^{1}/_{2}$ ft (2 m) high, slopes away more gently downstream for several hundred yards, and is lined with strong poles laid parallel to the sides of the valley.

The shape provides the strength to withstand the pressure of the vast lake of water that accumulates behind the dam. To deal with sudden floods and high water levels, sluices or spillways are built at each end of the dam to enable excess water to flow safely away. The dam's design and construction follow the same principles as those which go into building a man-made dam. It is an impressive piece of engineering and yet it is produced by a pair of beavers working purely by instinct.

They build their lodge in the middle of the artificial lake from a huge tangle of branches cemented together with mud from the lake bottom. An underwater entrance leads to one or sometimes two storeys above the water line: a hollowed-out feeding chamber below and another for sleeping above. Food for the winter is stored in the lake; this consists of saplings cut before they lose their leaves, which the beavers sink into the lake, often at the base of the dam. Like a natural refrigerator,

FOREST LODGE *Beavers
use branches from the
surrounding forest to
build their secure lodges.*

the near-freezing water below the ice keeps the food fresh. Even though thick snow and a layer of ice prevent the beavers from foraging in the surrounding countryside, they can swim out through their underwater tunnel, grab a fresh, green stalk and return under the ice to the lodge.

THE DAM BUILDERS

In the spring, when meltwater swells the feeder stream and the rain starts to fall, the lodge is in danger of flooding. But the beavers have an answer for that: they enlarge the spillways, and the flood waters escape downstream.

When the danger has passed, they build the sluices up again and adjust the height of the dam to ensure that at least 2 ft (60 cm) of water covers the base of the lodge. Any damage that has been caused

BLUEPRINT FOR A DAM *Before building a lodge, beavers have to construct a dam. First, they erect vertical poles and then fill in between them with a criss-cross of horizontally placed branches (right). They plug the gaps between the branches with a combination of weeds and mud (above) until the dam holds back sufficient water (below) to surround the lodge.*

HOW BEAVERS BUILD THEIR DAMS

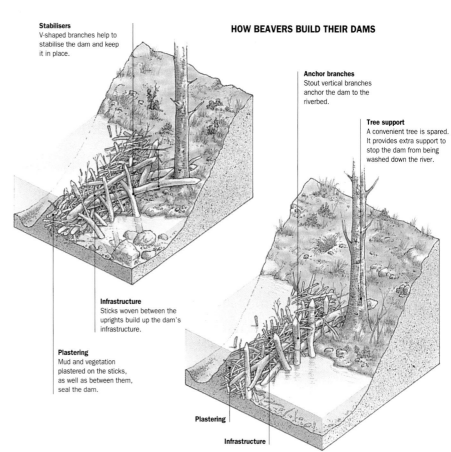

Stabilisers
V-shaped branches help to stabilise the dam and keep it in place.

Anchor branches
Stout vertical branches anchor the dam to the riverbed.

Tree support
A convenient tree is spared. It provides extra support to stop the dam from being washed down the river.

Infrastructure
Sticks woven between the uprights build up the dam's infrastructure.

Plastering
Mud and vegetation plastered on the sticks, as well as between them, seal the dam.

Plastering

Infrastructure

MOATED RESIDENCE *Once the beavers have constructed the dam and the artificial lake has filled up, they build a lodge of sticks, leaves and branches (bottom and top right). The lodge's entrance is under the water to deter predators such as foxes and wolves.*

Chimney
A vent lets heat and carbon dioxide escape.

Living space
The inside chamber, where the adults and 'kits' (young) spend much of the winter, is warm and dry.

Teamwork
All members of the family, including the kits, help to maintain the lodge and dam.

Insulation
Frozen mud between the sticks insulates the lodge in winter and protects it against predators.

Way in
The lodge's entrance is under water to reduce the risk of predators being able to get in.

Building materials
The fabric of the lodge is made from sticks and branches, together with mud and vegetation.

**BUILDING AND MAINTAINING
A BEAVER LODGE**

by the movement of the ice and the sudden influx of meltwater must be repaired. It is also a good time for parents to teach youngsters how to cut down and manipulate sticks.

A beaver's favourite food is wood bark from birch and aspen. If the forest has been cut back, so that the the supply of wood is farther away, the beavers dig canals down which they float their logs. The canals vary from 1 to 4 ft (0.3 to 1.2 m) in width and are up to 820 ft (250 m) long. In a single night an adult beaver can fell a tree, cut it into 3 to 10 ft (1 to 3 m) sections and float the logs down to the lake.

A beaver family gradually alters its environment to suit itself but the environment takes over in the end. Silt accumulates in the lake and the beavers, having lived in the same lodge and lake for several generations, have to move on and start all over again. Their lake turns first into a swamp and then, as it dries out, into flat grassland. In North America, human settlers built their homes alongside these rich meadows in the forest, and part of Montreal is built on just such a beaver-lake site.

ANIMAL KNOW-HOW

Many animals seem always to be in the right place at the right time for finding dinner. Some are wily opportunists, some rough pirates. Whatever their character, they all have the crucial 'know-how'.

The sparrow is a remarkable bird. Apparently 'insignificant' and extremely common, it has the ability to survive almost anywhere on Earth, adapting particularly well to living alongside people. And even though humans are changing the environment constantly, the sparrow has learned how to cope – not through any use of tools or by playing games – but by sheer 'know-how'.

The sparrow is not alone in the world of birds. The western gulls of the Farallon Islands, which lie in the Pacific Ocean to the west of San Francisco, are always on the lookout for feeding opportunities, but late in the year this takes a rather violent turn. The islands are home to breeding sea birds and seals. By November, the birds will have finished nesting and rearing, and are simply watching and waiting for their next meal. At the same time, the islands' elephant seals are just arriving to breed. The weather is unpredictable, and with winter setting in, conditions are likely to make fishing and scavenging difficult for the gulls. They line up on every vantage point and wait.

FOOD SCOUT *Gulls are always alert for feeding opportunities.*

Without any warning, they all take to the air and swoop down towards the sea. Nothing untoward has happened. There is no obvious cause for the exodus, and almost all that disturbs the surface calm is a bull elephant seal swimming slowly towards one of the island's beaches. He is an early arrival for the seal 'rookery' and is in pristine condition, ready to do battle with other bulls for the title of beach-master. But he is not alone in the water. Below and behind him a large, dark torpedo shape swims rapidly towards him. Suddenly, in a fountain of bloody froth, the huge seal disappears beneath the surface, and a big triangular fin and a thrashing tail take his place. The bull bobs up again, a 27 lb (12 kg) chunk of blubber missing from his ample rump. In another flurry of pink spray, the seal is dragged below once more, never to reappear. The gulls flock to the water where small slithers of blubber and fragments of skin litter the surface. They feed well.

Gulls are opportunists and quick to take advantage of an easy meal. In the Farallons they have learned to associate a fast-moving dark shape in the water with the prospect of food. They were ready to dine even before the attack took place. Whether one bird had spotted events unfolding and the information had passed in micro-seconds from one gull to another in a kind

of 'chorus line' is unknown. What they had shown, however, is that either individually or collectively, they had acquired 'know-how'.

Under the surface, meanwhile, another opportunist had also anticipated events. The dark shape was none other than a great white shark, the largest and most powerful predatory fish in the sea. The shark knew that bull elephant seals wallow in the waters off the Farallons each November and was simply waiting for an easy meal. At other times of the year, it probably hunts somewhere else, but somehow it was in the right place at the right time. The means by which that 'somehow' becomes shark 'know-how' is a mystery. Is it instinctive, or is it learned?

CALCULATED RISKS

Know-how is one way in which animals maximise their opportunities. An animal never knows for sure what is coming around the next corner. Nevertheless, it must make moment-to-moment decisions and is constantly having to make educated guesses about what best to do next. A western gull, for example, might well be faced with the following problem: is it better to wait for another shark attack, or should it try its luck at the fish market, or should it forsake feeding altogether and court a mate? If it chooses the fish market on a Sunday, it runs the risk of not feeding at all, if cast-off pickings are few that day. It might then return to an attack site after all the food has gone, and run the risk of losing its mate while it is away. The gull is

FOOD FOR KITTIWAKES Sea-bird colonies are information centres where incoming birds indicate to others where food is to be found.

unlikely to choose the least advantageous course of action, however, because animals usually get their priorities right. Although they are gamblers, the odds are stacked in their favour.

TAKING UP LODGINGS

There is the 'protection racket', for instance. Many animals take advantage of security services provided by others. Manx shearwaters and puffins know that cliff-top rabbit burrows on islands off the Welsh coast are good to nest in, if the rabbits have vacated them first.

In East Africa, pairs of lovebirds are attracted to the flutter of activity in an acacia tree, knowing that the huge communal nest hanging there belongs to a noisy gang of sociable weavers. They will provide the lovebirds with an early warning system and the protection they need to raise a family. So the lovebirds move into a vacated apartment and become tenants.

READY-MADE HOMES Puffins find refuge in abandoned cliff-top rabbit burrows.

Similarly, tufted ducks sometimes nest amongst mixed colonies of gulls and terns, benefiting not only from the sea birds' constant aerial surveillance, but also from their very effective use of mass mobbing to deter predators.

Know-how can also help animals to find the next meal. Foraging animals typically congregate in areas where they find the most food, but not all of them focus their attention there. Some animals spend a little of their time foraging in less favourable feeding sites, learning which would be the best if the main food source dried up unexpectedly. If resources remain the same, then these gamblers will lose. But in the wild, things change constantly and the animals that have gambled will be best prepared for change. They will have gained the 'know-how' – information for later use.

Information can be acquired in all sorts of ways. Sea birds such as guillemots, kittiwakes and fulmars live in great sea-cliff cities. There is a constant bustle of birds flying out to sea and returning from fishing expeditions. An individual only has to observe which birds return with full crops – the part of a bird's anatomy where it stores partly digested food – to know which direction to head in to make a successful catch. The colony is, in effect,

AT THE KILL *White-backed vultures spot others gathering around a carcass and come to join the feast.*

an information centre, and it saves birds from flying unnecessarily to parts of the ocean where the fishing is poor.

Something similar happens with East African vultures, which soar high in the air looking for dead or dying animals on which they can scavenge. But while they have one eye on the ground, the other is scanning the sky. As soon as one vulture spirals down to feed, others in the vicinity spot its descent and home in on the target too. They, in turn, are seen by others and the ripple of activity spreads out many miles around the corpse. Vultures have been known to arrive at a feeding site from up to 30 miles (50 km) away.

Watching for birds is not the exclusive

ON THE LOOKOUT *Minke whales locate schools of fish by watching for feeding sea birds.*

is moved slightly, then the nutcracker's efforts to relocate the store will be out by the same amount.

While Clark's nutcrackers, and a host of other, similar hoarders such as marsh tits and jays, rely on memory to relocate food, lammergeiers and oystercatchers rely on 'technique' to gain a meal. The lammergeier or bearded vulture lives mainly in Africa (with a few individuals in southern Europe) and is the poor relation among its fellow scavengers. It is last in the pecking order at carcasses, but it does not lose out since it has an appetite for the shards of bone and bone marrow that other vultures overlook. Bone

HIDDEN STORES *A Clark's nutcracker remembers the places where it hid pine seeds the previous summer.*

preserve of other birds, however. It can also be of great benefit to the most un-likely of animal observers. Minke whales 'spy-hop' – that is, they raise their heads out of the water and look about. A flock of birds at the surface is a sure sign that there is a shoal of fish below.

STORING FOOD FOR LEANER TIMES

Having found a food supply, some animals store it for leaner times, rather than simply living for the moment. This 'forethought' on their part is probably instinctive and built into an animal's genetic blueprint. It is known as 'caching', and it evolved in circumstances when all the birds that 'cached' their food survived, while those that did not died out.

The difficult thing about caching is to remember where the food is stored. This know-how is demonstrated by Clark's nutcracker, which lives in the mixed conifer forests of western North America. This is mountainous country where the higher slopes are covered in snow, even during the summer. Towards the end of summer, the birds harvest the seeds of piñon pines and fly several miles to suitable south-facing slopes, where the snow is less deep, to bury them.

Each nutcracker may bury as many as 33 000 pine seeds across a range of sites, each site containing four or five seeds – a huge number of sites for a small bird to re-member. It achieves this remarkable feat of memory by reference to local landmarks. Indeed, if a prominent object near a cache

HONORARY WOODPECKER

The aye-aye of Madagascar is one of the rarest primates in the world. Its most striking feature is a very long middle finger with which it extracts burrowing insect larvae from wood and pulp from fruits.

There are no woodpecker birds on Madagascar, and so the aye-aye – the origins of whose name are not known – has filled the vacant niche, behaving much like the bird. In its search for food, it taps gently on wood surfaces in order to locate cavities and to assess their contents – using what scientists believe might be a form of echolocation. It then bites into the soft wood with its sharp incisor teeth to open up the gallery and pokes its long finger in to extract the prize. Young aye-ayes learn at an early age from their mothers how to search for and extract insect larvae with their curious digit. They are clumsy at first, tapping everything they find, but with experience they gain dexterity.

PREYING FINGERS *The aye-aye's long, claw-like fingers enable it to winkle grubs from tree trunks (top). It uses the same technique on coconuts (bottom).*

WINTER RATIONS *European jays collect acorns and other nuts, which they hide for winter feeding.*

marrow is tender and nutritious, but unless some obliging hyena has broken the bones, it is exceedingly difficult to get out.

The lammergeier, however, has found a way. It grabs a long bone in its talons, flies high into the sky and drops the bone onto rocky ground beneath it. The bird's acute eyesight enables it to spot the site of the fall quickly and it immediately flies down to recover the pieces. In this way, the lammergeier satisfies much of its own nutritional requirements and certainly obtains all of the calcium needed by its developing youngsters.

LEARNING THE WAYS OF AN OYSTERCATCHER

The oystercatcher, one of the most familiar birds on the shorelines of Europe, relies on a different technique. It feeds on an extremely reliable source of food – beds of shellfish, such as mussels, razorfish and scallops – and has a long and pointed beak that, viewed from the front, is taller than it is wide, acting both as a wedge and as a lever. Nonetheless, it is one thing to possess such a tool for prising open a tightly clamped prey, and another to be able to use it. Oystercatchers, particularly young and inexperienced birds, must learn the technique by watching the more experienced birds in the flock.

Young oystercatchers have generally been brought up on farmland or in coastal areas that are very different from the places where mussels are found. The mussel bed or 'scar', as it is known in Britain, can be a daunting prospect for novices.

BONE MEAL *The lammergeier breaks open bones to feed on the marrow inside and pieces of the bone itself.*

When they arrive at the beds in late summer, young birds do not know how to isolate the most likely source of a meal from the millions of mussel shells that confront them on the shore. They waste valuable collecting time investigating empty shells or getting shells stuck on their beaks. If they are lucky, they plunder from adults or feed on leftover scraps. Then they begin to notice what the big birds are doing.

They watch adults wading into shallow water and stabbing at mussels that are open and still filtering food from the incoming tide. If a shell is slightly worn on one side from being battered by the waves, a bird knows stabbing at this weak point will bring success. Identifying vulnerable shells comes with experience. Birds tap shells before selecting them to find the ones that sound as if they are thinner. Although they learn a variety of techniques, most individuals have one preferred method and stick to it. There are stabbers who push the bill between the valves of the mussel, either left or right, and hammerers who smash the bill into one shell, consistently either the dorsal side or the ventral. Like-minded birds stick together, so that the method of shell-opening becomes significant not only in feeding but also in the selection of a mate.

By winter, the young birds have learned the all-important techniques and are becoming as proficient as the adults at opening mussels. Then comes a second period of learning. The adults, who have tolerated the presence of the young birds until now, change their behaviour: they attack any young competitors and steal from them mercilessly. The more canny and experienced adults rest between tides, but the hungry youngsters feed continuously, needing from 50 to 100 mussels a day in order to survive. To avoid interference from adults, they often head for estuaries to hunt for clams and for inland fields to find earthworms.

The following spring, all the birds return to the mussel beds and vie for a meal. The juvenile oystercatchers start by stabbing at mussel shells, but by the time they reach the age of three or four, about two-thirds of them will be hammering instead, the youngsters learning effective

A SCHOOL FOR CRACKING *Young North American black oystercatchers, like their European relatives, have to learn by example how to crack open shellfish.*

NATURE'S PIRATES OF THE AIR

Aerial piracy is rife among gulls, as well as among skuas, crows and some birds of prey. In a field study in Ireland, scientists watched the feeding behaviour of common gulls and black-headed gulls on a refuse tip. The larger common gulls soiled their bills very little, preferring to stand back and let their smaller relatives do all the foraging. Then, when a black-headed gull unearthed something that was larger than it could swallow in one go, the common gulls tried to relieve it of its food.

African fish eagles are not always the regal raptors that they seem. They rob kingfishers, pelicans, herons, ospreys and even their own young and their mates. For example, the fish eagle knows that the goliath heron, which wades out to depths that cannot be reached by other herons and stabs at fish with its enormous bill, catches the biggest fish. When the heron makes a catch, the eagle swoops in and grabs the prey before the heron can toss the fish into its mouth.

Animals living from thievery are known as kleptoparasites – 'parasites that steal'. Since this is a feeding strategy that obviously works, some species have resorted to piracy as a way of life. The frigate bird is the supreme aerial raider, able to snatch food from the sea's surface with the precision of a fraction of an inch and without pausing to reduce speed. However, when food is not readily available, it uses its aerial manoeuvrability to harass other coastal birds such as gannet-like boobies, who are no mean flyers themselves. The swashbuckling frigates rob the boobies with such alacrity that the victims are powerless to take any evasive action. The pirates pull their victims' tails and drive them into the sea until they regurgitate their catches. They even snatch food being passed from the hefty bill of an adult booby to its young – a feat that requires immaculate timing.

Aerial piracy is viable only if the bird does not expend too much energy, and it usually provides no more than a supplement to a broader diet. As a result, young pirates must learn to feed in more than one way. It takes time before a fledged frigate bird, for example, learns how to fly and manoeuvre in the sky so that it joins the ranks of nature's flying corsairs.

EAGLE THIEFS *Bald eagles are not averse to stealing food from other eagles.*

techniques from watching parents and other adults. Learning and experience supplement the birds' innate knowledge, to play a large part in their survival.

FINE ART OF CHEATING

Animals also cheat in order to acquire food. Some of the most cunning scoundrels of the bird world are a couple of South American antbirds – the white-winged shrike tanager and the bluish-slate ant shrike. Both masquerade as upstanding pillars of avian society, acting as trusty lookouts in the constant war with predators.

The birds are amongst a menagerie of animals that follow columns of marauding army ants. These ferocious ants flush insects such as juicy grasshoppers and katydids from the undergrowth and the birds following behind snatch them as best they can. There are many species of ant bird, and each one has its place in the pecking order. Dominant birds fly ahead of the ants, collecting the best prey, while lesser ones take positions on the side and to the rear. In the trees above, a procession of other birds follows, relying on the 'sentinel' services of the ant birds. Ant birds tend to be more alert for predators and are the first birds to spot a swooping hawk. All the others depend on the ant birds' screams to raise the alarm.

The ant shrike and the shrike tanager, however, take advantage of their privileged position to cheat their competitors. If a grasshopper jumps from the grass and a rival bird is about to snatch it, the ant bird gives a false alarm call. The other bird is startled, and since it would rather lose an insect than its life, it takes evasive action. The cheat, meanwhile, scoops up the prey. For these two ant birds, cheating pays.

STRATEGIES FOR SURVIVAL

3

JOINT VENTURE *White pelicans in the Mississippi Delta work together to catch fish.*

MANY ANIMALS FARE MORE SUCCESSFULLY AS PART OF A TEAM. COOPERATIVE HUNTERS ACHIEVE BETTER RESULTS THAN AN ANIMAL ON ITS OWN WOULD, AND SEVERAL PAIRS OF ALERT EYES ARE A GOOD DEAL MORE EFFICIENT AT SPOTTING DANGER AND RAISING THE ALARM THAN ONE. 'SAFETY IN NUMBERS' IS AS TRUE OF THE ANIMAL WORLD AS OF THE HUMAN WORLD. ANOTHER CRUCIAL SURVIVAL STRATEGY IS FORWARD PLANNING, BASED ON ACCURATE ANTICIPATION OF EVENTS SUCH AS THE SEASONAL BLOOMING OF FOOD PLANTS OR THE ANNUAL GATHERING TOGETHER OF CERTAIN KINDS OF PREY. AND IF ALL OTHER SURVIVAL STRATEGIES FAIL, AN ANIMAL CAN SOMETIMES RESORT TO A VERY HUMAN ATTRIBUTE — IT CAN CHEAT.

WHALE HUNT *Humpback whales round up shoals of krill.*

WORKING TOGETHER

Huge humpback whales have to work in teams to herd enough tiny krill to make a worthwhile meal. And a pack of small hunting dogs, by working cooperatively, can bring down a large wildebeest.

The hunters – five experienced and one apprentice – assemble quietly on the forest floor. With no more than a nod or a shake of the head to coordinate their movements, they take up their positions. The quarry, a troop of colobus monkeys sitting high in a tree nonchalantly chewing on leaves and sucking at fruit, is unaware of the preparations below.

The monkeys are about to be driven into an ambush, but so far they remain oblivious to the danger. They see the youngest of the hunters slowly climb one of the trees behind them, but it appears to be doing no harm, although it is just worrying enough for the monkeys to become a little unsettled.

Meanwhile, two other members of the hunting team have outflanked the colobus troop, and are ready to take up positions on either side of it. They will prevent any monkeys from escaping. Another, the most experienced of the hunters, silently overtakes the prey and climbs a tree ahead of them, a move they do not notice. The two remaining hunters make ready to charge.

With loud screams, the two attackers shin up the trees. The flankers crash noisily through the branches and the startled colobus monkeys bolt. They leap nimbly from tree to tree and make their escape down the avenue between the two flankers. Then the hunters play their trump card. The ambusher ahead of the troop leaps from cover. The fleeing colobus hesitate, then panic, giving the attackers time to catch up with them. Immediately they

HUNTING PARTY
A posse of chimps chases colobus monkeys through the treetops.

MALES FIRST *Lionesses (top) hunt cooperatively. Once the prey is caught, however, it is the male lions (bottom) who have first pick at the carcass.*

grab a victim, and then another. The hunters cry out as they grab the prey, and a growing band of spectators on the forest floor below joins in. The hunt is a success.

The hunters in this clever and well-coordinated attack are chimpanzees. They find their quarry in the Thai Forest of the Ivory Coast, and the fact that they hunt has changed our view of the chimpanzee as a relatively harmless, fruit-eating creature. It also suggests how our ancestors might have obtained food – the kind of teamwork which, many thousands of years later, enabled us to work together to achieve our dominant place in nature. Hunting alone, no chimpanzee would have been able to catch a nimble colobus, but hunting together in a highly organised team and using the twin tactics of surprise and confusion, the hunting group was rewarded with a protein-rich meal of monkey meat.

In order to achieve this degree of co-ordination, members of the group needed to 'talk' to each other. Communication is the key to cooperation, and cooperation is the key to successful hunting.

HUNTING WITH THE PRIDE

Most social predators have their own 'languages', using channels of communication appropriate to their best-developed senses. Lions, for example, rely on sight, smell and sound, whereas army ants communicate using touch, vibration, smell and taste. By talking to its team-mates, an individual recognises its status in the group and learns the role it must play. In order to work together effectively, a hunting team must ensure that squabbles are minimised. And successful teamwork brings its rewards. A solitary lion, for example, catches its prey in only 15 per cent of chases (one in seven), whereas a small pride of half a dozen animals has a 32 per cent success rate (one in three). By working in a group, a lion doubles its chances of eating.

The hunt itself often begins at sunset. The lionesses in the pride peer out from a vantage point on a grassy knoll, their fawn coats blending with the dry savannah vegetation, only the flick of an ear giving away their position. They watch quietly but intently as a ragged line of wildebeests shuffle by in their relentless search for pastures new. The lions identify their victim by its difference from the rest – a gangly youngster, an infirm old-timer, or an animal with a limp, a clear signal of vulnerability. The males in the pride take little part in hunting. Their job is to protect the lionesses and their cubs from other prides of lions and from hyenas.

Moving swiftly and silently, one of the lionesses leaves the group and uses a gully to reach the other side of the herd unnoticed. This flanking movement will cut off their escape. Meanwhile the rest of the pride begins to creep on their bellies towards the nearest wildebeests. They fan out, keeping low, their statuesque heads rock steady, their eyes locked on to the target. A mother wildebeest feeding a calf looks up, alert to the merest whiff of scent. The hunting team freeze.

Reaching her position, the flanking lioness squats down and waits. The rest of the pride creep slowly forward – the hunters must get to within 100 ft (30 m) of their victim – and then suddenly they bolt from cover. The wildebeests run this way and that in a cloud of panic. The lions reach full speed, about 36 mph (58 km/h), but they can only keep this up for a short distance. It is almost over already. The target animal – a large old bull – has been isolated from the rest of the herd. It is driven straight into the path of the flanking lioness. Cuffing the wildebeest's hind legs away with a powerful thwack of its paw, the predator trips up the prey, and goes in for the kill.

The lioness grabs the panting wildebeest by the neck, constricting its windpipe and suffocating it. The rest of the pride pile in, ripping at the soft underside. The large males appear from nowhere, and, after an unruly bout of snarling and swiping, they take the first sitting. When they have had their fill, it is the turn of the hunters – the lionesses. The cubs then feast on the scraps – if they are not disturbed, that is. The ambush has been successful, but as often as not there are other

JOINT EFFORT *By hunting together, lionesses can bring down prey, such as an adult wildebeest, that is larger than they are.*

POWER IN NUMBERS *Coyotes hunt more successfully in twos and threes than when alone.*

inhabitants of the plains ready to lift a hard-earned carcass.

Rival teams, and scavengers such as hyenas and vultures, wait in the wings to appropriate a lion's prize. Lions may be large and powerful, but a pack of noisy hyenas is more than a match for a lion hunting alone. Cooperation, therefore, not only contributes to a successful hunt, but also enables the hunters to keep their food from marauders.

There is, however, a price to be paid for this success. The disadvantage of hunting cooperatively is that food has to be shared. As a result, each individual in the group receives less from a kill than if it hunted alone. Some predators, such as North American coyotes, have it both ways.

They hunt singly when the prey, such as rodents and squirrels, is small or plentiful, but pursue animals communally – usually parents accompanied by their offspring – when the prey is scarce or large.

STAMINA AND SPEED

Hunting in a closely coordinated pack, African wild dogs are able to tackle prey ten times the size of each dog. The hunt takes place mainly at dawn or dusk, but a pack may be active on a cloudless, moonlit night or during an overcast day when the midday sun is hidden behind clouds. On the flat savannah, the dogs rely on sight to spot their prey – an antelope or zebra. Like many predators, they look for the weak, the deformed and the young, spotting the telltale signs that one animal might be easier to overhaul than another.

The hunt starts at a trot. Unlike other plains predators, the dogs rely on stamina and sheer determination. Once they have chosen their quarry and isolated it from the herd, they keep after it, wearing it down until they judge the time is right to make the kill. To tire the prey, a couple of the pursuing team keep on its heels while the rest of the pack jog comfortably along, fanning out behind.

As the first chasers tire, they fall back and another pair take their place. This relay pattern is repeated time and again, the dogs driving the prey along constantly at speeds up to 44 mph (70 km/h) for

more than 3 miles (5 km). Eventually, worn down by a combination of tiredness and terror, the prey slows. In an instant, perceiving somehow that the end is near, the chaser dogs bring the unfortunate victim to a sudden halt, one grabbing the tail and the other latching on to the sensitive lips. The rest of the pack catches up, each dog throwing itself at the flanks and belly, weakening the prey still further through loss of blood.

A large zebra provides food for all, and there will be some left over for the

THE KILL *African hunting dogs chase and hold down their prey.*

hangers-on – vultures, marabou storks and jackals – that invariably accompany a feast of this kind. Smaller prey, such as impala, would be demolished in less than ten minutes, and not a scrap would be left.

Waiting at the den site are the cubs. They greet the returning hunters enthusiastically, running up to an adult and licking its face. This behaviour causes the dog to regurgitate some meat – an automatic response over which it has no control. By the time they are three months old, the young hunting dogs are able to accompany the hunt. Watching and learning, they pick up the vital hunting skills from their parents and the rest of the pack. Eventually they, too, will play their role in a well-disciplined and well-coordinated communal hunt.

UNDERSEA HUNTING

Many predatory mammals gang together in hunting groups in order to obtain their food: hyenas, wolves and dingoes on land, and dolphins and killer whales at sea. Even the enormous baleen whales occasionally cooperate. Humpback whales, for instance, must feed well and fast during the brief

polar summer, because they do not feed at all for more than six months during their migrations north and south and while in their winter breeding grounds in the tropics. In order to maximise their catches, therefore, they have developed an ingenious method of herding small fish and krill known as 'bubble-netting'.

One whale dives deep below a large shoal of small fish and swims in a circle, blowing bubbles as it goes. The bubbles rise to the surface, forming a cylindrical curtain that traps the fish in the middle. Flashes of light reflecting from the bubbles frighten the fish, which withdraw into a dense mass. With a sonorous moan and the occasional squeak, the humpback alerts other whales and five or six might collaborate in the bubble-blowing. A communal

WHALE-FULL *A humpback whale, its throat swollen with a soup of fish and seawater, surfaces in a bubble net.*

PELICAN FOOD *White pelicans feed in a U-shaped formation designed to herd fish into the shallows.*

bubble net might be up to 72 ft (22 m) in diameter. The whales then swim rapidly up through the middle of the cylinder with their mouths open and burst through the

surface, their mouths filled with a concentrated soup of fish and sea water. Squeezing the water out through their baleen plates, they then swallow their catch of fish.

Several species of sea birds also go fishing together, relying not on a specialised technique but on sheer weight of numbers. Like their gigantic humpback neighbours, blue-eyed shags feast in the nutrient-rich waters of the Southern Ocean.

They form huge rafts on the sea's surface by swimming in close formation, and as they move along, each bird occasionally dips its head below the surface, searching for fish. As soon as a shoal is located, the birds dive below and give chase. In the confusion few fish escape. A fish might avoid the stabbing beak of one shag, only to swim straight into that of another swimming alongside. By hunting cooperatively, the birds give themselves a better chance of spotting and catching food in the vast, featureless ocean.

The great white pelicans of South America also gather in large hunting groups, but in shallow water. Lining up side by side, or in circular or horseshoe-shaped flotillas, the birds herd shoals of fish into natural cul-de-sacs along the shore. Unable to escape, the fish are scooped up in the pelicans' enormous bills as they dip their heads below the surface in unison. The technique is well coordinated, each member of the group benefiting from the actions of its neighbours.

SAFETY IN NUMBERS

Cooperation can also benefit the prey. An individual in a shoal, flock or herd is less likely to be picked off than an animal on its own, although a group of prey animals confronted by bubble-blowing whales or a coordinated wolf pack is at a serious disadvantage. However, a predator hunting alone among prey that lives in a group is likely to be spotted by the many pairs of

STOCKADE *Musk oxen face predators such as wolves with a protective wall of horns.*

watchful eyes. Among a flock of feeding ostriches or geese, for example, there are always one or two birds looking out for danger while the others feed. And if a lone predator does get close enough to attack, it is likely to be flummoxed by the criss-crossing of panicking animals to such an extent that they all escape.

Some animals have cooperative defence strategies. Under attack by Arctic wolves, a herd of musk oxen forms itself into a protective phalanx – the youngsters surrounded by a ring of adults, all with their horns facing outwards. Similarly, elephants confront danger with a wall-like formation, adults lining up in front of their babies. At the head of the herd is the huge matriarch, flapping her great ears and trumpeting loudly.

PEEKING DUCKS — KEEPING AN EYE OPEN

Animals are at risk at night. Birds seek safety by roosting on ledges, or in trees, reeds or bushes. Always alert for nocturnal predators such as owls, they do not sleep continuously, but occasionally open one eye and 'peek'. The more birds roosting together, the less often an individual needs to peek.

In one study on the banks of the River Thames near Oxford, a group of roosting ducks was observed each night sleeping on an old jetty. The ducks closer to the shore, and to danger, peeked much more than those at the end of the jetty. With several birds between them and a

predator approaching from land, the chances are that birds at the end of the jetty would be caught last. They therefore peeked less.

GOOSE ALERT *Like sleeping ducks, Canada geese keep a constant eye open for danger, even when resting.*

travel many miles to a cleaning station for a 'wash and brush-up', and there is some evidence to suggest that cleaners – either fish or shrimps – are vital to the health of the reef community. In places where cleaners have been removed, the larger fish succumb to various fungal diseases and there is a noticeable decline in fish stocks.

One fish, though, has taken advantage of this temporary lull in predatory activity on the part of the bigger fish. The false cleaner looks like a cleaner fish, bobs about like a cleaner fish and hangs out at cleaning stations, but any grouper attended by this impostor will be in for an unpleasant surprise. Lying motionless in the water expecting the soothing attentions of its usual cleaners, the large fish is rudely awakened when the false cleaner darts in and bites off a chunk of its fin.

Some species of false cleaner, such as the saw-toothed blenny, have even been known to bite people swimming in the vicinity of a cleaning station.

By grouping together, prey animals can also go on the offensive. Songbirds, threatened by an owl or a hawk, gather into noisy gangs and mob the predator until it moves away; crows mob buzzards; and terns and gulls dive-bomb intruders that have strayed too close to their nests. There is, however, the danger that a predator will turn on the mob and grab one of its members. Buzzards are quite capable of flying upside-down for long enough to catch an unwary mobster flying overhead. The flock must approach close enough to harass the predator, but not so close that one of its members is caught.

STRANGE PARTNERSHIPS

Occasionally there is a truce between predator and potential prey. Small fish can be useful to bigger fish in ways other than as food. At special sites on coral reefs or at seamounts, large fish such as groupers, manta rays and sharks line up at cleaning stations to be attended to by small cleaner fish such as wrasses or gobies, which are identified by a blue stripe down the side of

an elongated body and a particular bobbing way of swimming. The large predator forsakes its predatory instincts as the cleaners pick off parasites, scraps of food and dead scales. The relationship between host and cleaner has evolved to such an extent that the cleaners are able to enter the mouth and gill chambers of the host without coming to any harm. Some fish

CLEANING UP *Grouper fish attend 'cleaning stations' where they are groomed by cleaner wrasses.*

FORESIGHT OR PROGRAMMING?

In temperate lands, animals use the bounty of a plentiful summer to anticipate winter shortages. Either they build up external food stores, or they put on internal stores of fat before hibernating.

The ability to antici-pate lean times is essential for sur-viving in the wild. Whether animals other than humans are able to do so consciously is a moot point, but a considerable number of them store food during times of plenty for use when times are hard.

What makes an animal store food rather than eat it immediately is unclear, but the amount of food available at a par-ticular moment is likely to influence a creature's behaviour, as is the time of year. The North American deer mouse, for in-stance, starts to hoard more food when the temperature drops and the days shorten in the autumn. With the relatively lean months of winter approaching, the deer mouse has gained an advantage over any competitors that do not hoard food, and is therefore more likely to survive and breed. It is an example of natural selection in action.

BURIED TREASURE

The wholesale slaughter of a farmer's laying hens by a fox is another example of such a survival strategy. When a red fox breaks into a chicken coop, it is suddenly confronted with a glut of food. Its natural reaction is to kill as many chickens as possible, not for reasons of blood lust, but to collect the food while it is abundant in order to store it for later. If undisturbed, the fox would bury its prey at several different places throughout its territory, returning to the caching sites to recover the corpses when hunting was poor.

Similar behaviour has been seen in the cat family – when caracals, leopards and snow leopards kill sheep, and lions slaugh-ter cattle. In the wild, lions make multiple kills during cooperative hunts and lynxes make multiple kills of hares. Excess food is 'cached' – that is, it is covered with grass, leaves, earth or any available loose material. During the northern winter, lynxes cache the snowshoe hares in snow, hiding each carcass in a different place.

Scatter-hoarding, as this type of behaviour is known, has been developed by many crea-tures, including birds such as crows, jays, nuthatches, titmice and nutcrackers, and mammals such as foxes and squirrels. The cached food may be ani-mal or vegetable, but consists most commonly of seeds and nuts, which remain edible for a long time. The grey squirrel, for example, buries nuts in holes in the ground that it carefully disguises with a cover-ing of dead leaves and other vegetation. The African ground

INSURANCE *The red fox will bury some of its catch of ptarmigan and ground squirrel for leaner times.*

STOCKING UP *The lynx may kill several hares at one time and store a few for later.*

squirrel collects seeds, digs a hole and then hammers the seeds into the earth using its incisor teeth; it pushes soil over the hole with its forepaws and disguises the site with a well-placed leaf.

The North American nutcracker, which has even developed a special pouch under its chin in which to transport food, buries pine kernels on the south-facing slopes of hillsides. Only a little snow accumulates here during the winter and it melts early in spring, giving the nutcracker access to its larder just as its youngsters are hatching.

Scatter-hoarders have to remember where all their sites are located, and they do this by reference to the landmarks near each of them. By using several sites spread out over a wide area, these animals reduce the amount of food they might lose to opportunists who happen to stumble upon their caches. Also, by hiding the food in different types of site, scatter-hoarders make it harder for any attentive thief that watches them at work to find all the places where they store their food.

Theft is not a scatter-hoarder's only problem. North American grey squirrels feed on acorns from both red and white oaks, which germinate at different times. The acorns of the red oak lie dormant throughout the winter, germinating in the spring, and their acorns make ideal food for winter storage.

The acorns of the white oak, on the other hand, germinate immediately, sending down a large taproot, although they grow very little until the spring. Squirrels seem not to like taproots or seedlings, because they deal with white-oak acorns in

LARDER RAIDS *A red squirrel may visit its different caches for years to come.*

a special way before caching them. The squirrels bite out the seed embryo, effectively killing the acorn and preventing it from germinating.

WINTER LARDERS

Not all squirrels, though, are scatter-hoarders. Pine squirrels and Douglas' squirrels in North American coniferous forests cut cones from the trees, causing them to fall to the ground. A squirrel might harvest many cones from a tree before moving on to the next. It then takes the cones one by one, or occasionally two at a time, to stores called 'middens', which can be recognised by the piles of cone scales and other debris left over from winter feasting. These storage sites are used year after year, each pile containing 20 or so buried cones. The middens are cold and damp, so the cones do not open. They are therefore preserved indefinitely, and the kernels inside are protected by the hard outer scales from the attentions of thieving birds and mice. The squirrels, which are highly territorial, defend their middens from any intruders.

This form of caching, in which a single large cache is collected and stored, is known as larder-hoarding and is also practised by acorn woodpeckers, bees and

HOME IN THE HEDGES *A wood mouse hoards nuts and berries in its hedgerow store.*

many small rodents. Wood mice, voles and chipmunks, for example, store seeds and nuts in a separate chamber in the home burrow. An African pouched rat's nest was found with 1383 seeds of the Mwabve tree, plus a large quantity of dried grass seeds, weighing in all around 2½ lb (1.2 kg); as the rat can carry only eight Mwabve seeds at a time, that part of the cache alone represented more than 170 excursions.

Similarly, the nest burrows of Eurasian mole rats have been found with over 110 lb

HONEY SWEET *The honeypot ant's abdomen is filled with honey dew.*

(50 kg) of stored food in special chambers. Bumblebees make storage 'jars' in which they put the pollen and nectar collected from flowers in the neighbourhood. And Australian honeypot ants have living storage jars. Specially chosen workers hang from the roof of one of the underground galleries, their abdomens grossly swollen with stored honeydew.

In the US and Mexico, acorn woodpeckers drill hundreds of evenly spaced holes in dead tree trunks and fill each space with an acorn. Where forests have been cleared to make way for human settlements, the birds take to drilling holes in telegraph poles.

A single-site larder is much easier to raid than a scattered hoard, and larder-hoarders defend their food stores vigorously. Acorn woodpeckers chase away any potential thief, including devious fox squirrels and any other acorn woodpeckers. Scatter-hoarders have a

different problem. Even though their hoarding sites are widely scattered, a determined thief is able to raid their caches if it follows their every move. In this way, willow tits have been known to follow coal tits and then rob them of their caches, and crows find the caches left by jays.

MEAT SAFE

Some animals store their food for relatively short periods, collecting the food one day and eating it a day or two later. The aptly named 'butcher-birds' – members of the shrike family – for example, do not simply cache items of food, they impale them on long thorns, creating a macabre larder for all to see. Shaped somewhat like stocky little hawks, they are very active hunters, constantly on the lookout for prey. It is thought that they catch food more quickly than they can devour it, hence the larder.

Other birds of prey that conceal food for later consumption include goshawks in California and sparrowhawks in Britain, which have been seen to keep a larder in the crook of a tree or in bushes. A female sparrowhawk, for instance, was spotted one winter with a jackdaw that it had caught. After plucking and eating some of its kill, it hid the rest of the carcass in bushes and returned five times to finish it off. Small hawks and falcons are vulnerable to sneak thieves and they, too, store unfinished meals in safe larders.

In east Africa, the solitary leopard suffers from pilfering. Its hard-earned kill attracts vultures, which in turn alert hyenas and lions that there is food to be had. The

SPIKED *The rufous-backed shrike impales its locust prey on a thorn.*

leopard's answer is to drag the carcass up a tree. Here the food is safe from other hunters, which enables the leopard to take advantage of a period of good hunting without the risk of losing the food it has

OUT OF REACH *A leopard stores its leftovers high in a tree.*

already caught. The availability of prey fluctuates with the seasons; it is rarely plentiful and sometimes scarce, and a tree larder provides a short-term insurance policy. It has been estimated that leopards haul over half their kills into trees.

Hyenas, known popularly as the 'garbage collectors' of the savannah, are powerful and well-coordinated hunters. Presented with a superabundance of food, they too indulge in multiple kills, and on one occasion in South Africa a pack was observed dispatching more than 100 gazelles in one night. Torrential rain had prevented the prey from escaping and the hyenas made the most of the opportunity, feasting on some of the carcasses and caching the others. Hyenas tend to drag their food into cool, underwater larders, where it is safer from scavengers and is less likely to go off.

One major problem with stored meat in hot climates is the speed with which it putrefies. Animals tend to avoid rotting flesh, but if no other food is available then they have to make do with putrid meat. Elsewhere, however, the icy temperatures and the snow and ice found at high latitudes or in high mountain ranges provides animals with a natural freezer. A frozen moose carcass in Yellowstone National Park can feed a small pack of hungry coyotes for several weeks.

Caching in snow can be a matter of life and death for some creatures, but the freezing temperatures have their drawbacks, too. On the one hand, the cold preserves the animal's dead tissue, which might otherwise decay, but on the other it presents the hoarder with a problem – how to defrost the meal. The great horned owl of the Americas has a solution: it sits on a frozen carcass, thawing it out and consuming it bit by bit.

Animals have various ways of keeping their food fresh. Coal tits store caterpillars by removing the head and gut, and hoard aphids by compacting 20 to 50 of them into a small storable pellet. Moles like fresh meat and so remove the rear end of any worms they have caught in order to keep them alive – but unable to escape – in underground larders.

American pine and red squirrels favour dehydrated foods, which have the advantage of lasting longer. They collect mushrooms and leave them on a branch to dry before caching them for the winter. One pine squirrel living in a lodgepole pine forest in the Rockies was once observed

cutting through a large *Cortinarius* fungus by gnawing at the stalk and then dragging it back to the base of a tree. The mushroom-shaped fungus was almost as big as the squirrel, so the animal gnawed it into manageable chunks and carried them to its cache high in the tree.

BODY FAT

An alternative to caching is to carry your food on you. Many animals have a good feed in times of plenty and put on body fat that can be burned up to provide energy when times are hard. Humpback whales must cram all their feeding into a couple of months because they fast for most of the year. During the winter months, they mate and give birth to their young in the tropics where there is insufficient food to sustain them. In order to stock up, they swim thousands of miles to nutrient-rich polar or temperate seas each summer and consume vast amounts of krill and small fish. The food is stored as blubber.

Smaller migrants, such as songbirds, must anticipate the start of their migration

SALMON FEAST *Alaskan brown bears congregate at rapids (top) where they can more easily catch salmon swimming upriver (right).*

and put on sufficient weight to fuel the journey. Some birds, such as the waders from South America that fly all the way to the Arctic to breed, stop off at traditional refuelling stations along the way. One such stop-off point is in Delaware Bay on the east coast of the United States, where the migrants arrive just as the horseshoe crabs leave the sea to deposit their eggs on the shore. The waders have a feeding bonanza on the eggs before continuing their flight north. One very small migrant, the rufous hummingbird of the west coast of North America, has its route so well worked out that it always arrives at refuelling stops at the exact moment when its favourite flowers open.

Other animals do not migrate to avoid the bad weather, but hibernate instead.

They, too, must stock up for the winter. The grizzly bears of North America feast well on summer berries and fruits, but have an almost foolproof way of putting on weight for the winter – they go fishing. Each year the rivers of the Pacific coast run with salmon returning to their home rivers to spawn. At vantage points such as rapids and small waterfalls along the rivers, the bears congregate in large numbers. They suppress their natural tendency to fight each other and instead hook out salmon after salmon, quickly putting on the fat that they need to sustain them through the cold winter months.

RAISING THE ALARM

Alarm calls are more than sudden exclamations of fear. For higher animals, they convey meaning, much like human words. The call may identify a predator, and even indicate a means of escape.

The vervet monkeys of east Africa are vulnerable in the open: a large constricting snake such as the African python might slither undetected into a position close to the troop and seize a young monkey; a leopard might creep within striking distance and pounce on an adult; and a martial eagle or a crowned hawk eagle might swoop out of the sky and grab a victim before it has time to escape. Vervets therefore have to stay alert when foraging on the ground.

Like many monkeys, vervet monkeys are great conversationalists, chattering away almost continuously. They grunt and squeak, flash their eyelids, groom, kiss, gesture and grimace – all components of a rich and complex body language. They also have a system of interesting and effective alarm calls.

When a troop of monkeys are feeding on the ground, one or two members of the troop are always looking about for signs of danger. Their different alarm calls trigger different reactions. If a leopard approaches, the sentinel gives a loud bark and the rest of the troop flee to the treetops. If a martial eagle is spotted soaring overhead, a loud chuckle sends everyone into the bushes. The monkeys' choice of escape is a direct response to the hunting pattern of the predators. Leopards hunt by stealth, using bushes as cover and taking their victims by surprise; they can take monkeys on the ground or in bushes, but are not nimble enough to catch them in the topmost branches of trees. The eagle, on the other hand, can pluck a monkey from the ground or from a tree, and so the safest place during an eagle attack is a thick bush.

Snakes are greeted by a third alarm call. A high-pitched chattering stimulates each member of the troop to stand up on its hind legs and look around carefully for the danger in the grass. Sometimes they mob the intruder; at other times they simply stay clear. As long as they can see it, they are safe. There are also distinctive alarm calls to warn of baboons, which sometimes attack vervets, and in some regions there is even a specific alarm for man, the most feared of all predators.

VERVET-SPEAK

Until recently it was thought that animal alarm calls were simply a general manifestation of fear, but studies of vervet monkeys have shown that – even without the actual predator in sight – each alarm call means something so specific to the monkeys that it is almost like a 'word'. A vervet word

RED ALERT *A vervet monkey gives the snake alarm call (left). A big cat in the vicinity triggers the leopard alarm call (right).*

might not be as precise as a human word; it might be that an eagle alarm refers, on the one hand, to any recognised bird of prey, or, on the other hand, to specific escape instructions. Similarly, the leopard

---

ANT ALARM SMELLS

Ants have no alarm calls, but they do discharge alarm smells or pheromones. Wood ants spray a mixture of formic acid with a special alarm pheromone: the acid repels invaders and the pheromone summons support. The signal radiates outwards over about 2½ in (6 cm) in 13 seconds, and fades out in about 35 seconds. In that time others of the colony pick up the scent and join in the attack. As more ants release the pheromone, the signal spreads out through the colony and in a short time an entire army is mobilised.

---

alarm might simply mean 'spotted cat', or it could mean 'run to the trees'. Whatever turns out to be the correct translation, the interesting thing to scientists studying these monkeys is that the sound they make represents a particular object or course of action in the external world, a form of behaviour thought, at one time, to be confined to humankind.

The investigations did not stop there, for there was another question that had to be asked: is this ability to use what scientists have called 'protowords' innate or learned? When adult vervets give the leopard alarm, it is almost always for leopards, although lions, hyenas, cheetahs and jackals sometimes elicit the same call. Martial and crowned hawk eagles are the usual recipients of the eagle alarm, but black-chested snake eagles and tawny eagles – both capable of snatching a young vervet – also trigger the eagle call.

The snake alarm, though primarily used for pythons, is also given for cobras, mambas and puff adders. To our ears, the alarm calls made for these different snakes sound the same; they are described as high-pitched chutters. But there may be subtle variations between the snake alarms for constricting snakes and the ones for poisonous snakes.

Infant vervets are not so particular about the way in which they use alarm calls. They give leopard alarms for warthogs, eagle alarms for pigeons and snake alarms for tortoises. One small and misguided individual even screamed an eagle alarm for a falling leaf. But these alarm calls, even from a baby vervet's youngest days, are not entirely random. Leopard alarms are only given in response to animals on the ground. The snake alarm is given for anything that resembles a snake, including vines. Infant vervets, it seems, start life with a predisposition to give alarm calls to a broad class of predators but subsequently narrow the field down to those that matter. Adults, particularly mothers, teach them how to respond to alarm calls, and also which creatures are predators and which are not.

If an infant gives an alarm call, such as an eagle alarm for a pigeon, the adults in the troop look up, see the harmless bird, and do nothing. If the youngster spots a martial eagle, the others look up, see the eagle and give the eagle alarm themselves while urging their offspring to run for cover. The adults' response reinforces the infant's behaviour.

In an experiment in which recorded alarm calls were played back on a tape recorder to a group of vervets in Kenya, the scientists waited until a very young vervet became separated from its mother, and then played the eagle alarm. The youngster was initially confused, looking this way and that, searching for its mother in order to find out what to do. Eventually it ran to the safety of her arms. The adult, meanwhile had been giving the infant many clues about the way in which it should behave.

The experiment was repeated a few days later, and in the intervening time the infant had learned a lot. The scientists used video cameras to record what happened and a frame-by-frame analysis of the tape revealed what the infant had been taught. It heard the call, looked immediately towards its mother, saw her looking skywards, and then looked into the sky itself. A few weeks later, the young vervet's immediate response to an alarm call was to look directly into the sky.

VARYING THE CALL

As they grow older, infant vervets appear to sharpen their responses to different classes of predators, and learn to associate different alarm calls not only with specific predators but also with particular escape strategies. Furthermore, they can adapt the nature of their alarm calls and their responses according to the hunting behaviour of the predators. In the tropical forests of Cameroon in west Africa, for example, vervet monkeys may be hunted by people with dogs. Unlike their savannah-based relatives, who make a lot of noise when threatened by a predator, these forest-living monkeys give soft, high-pitched alarm calls at a frequency that blends with

PASSING ON THE MESSAGE
Superb starlings warn vervet monkeys of approaching danger.

the general background noise of the forest. This makes them difficult to detect from the ground below, although the monkeys themselves can pick out the calls clearly from all the other sounds. They then flee silently into the dense foliage where humans with dogs cannot follow.

Vervet monkeys also listen for the alarm calls of other species. The east

African troops share their savannah home with superb starlings, which, like the vervets, feed mainly on the ground under acacia trees. The monkeys ignore the general chirruping and chattering and the starlings' sustained warbling song, but react instantly to an alarm call. The starlings have two alarm calls – one for aerial predators and another for hunters approaching on the ground.

Aerial attacks are most likely to come from small hawks and falcons, and are of no interest to the vervets, but the ground predators may well be a shared threat. The monkeys ignore the starlings' aerial alarm call, but respond to the ground-predator alarm: they stop foraging and look about for the source of danger. This means that infant vervets must therefore learn starling language, too.

PLAYING BACK THE PYTHON

In another playback experiment, a researcher presented a troop of monkeys with a starling alarm call that was given in response to an approaching python. Young monkeys between 23 and 84 days old recognised the call as being significant and looked up, but they did not know what to do. At 120 days, however, they had learned from the adults to stop feeding and look about; some panicked and shot up the nearest tree.

But how far, the scientists wondered, could this seemingly intelligent behaviour be taken? Although the monkeys had been able to recognise the link between the calling behaviour of other animals and danger, could they appreciate the presence of a predator from other danger signals when there were no alarm calls or alarm behaviour? Leopards, for instance, hoist their hard-won prey into a tree to avoid the attentions of scavenging lions or hyenas, so a larder of this type is a sure sign that a leopard is nearby.

The researchers chanced upon a gazelle carcass, placed it in a tree and watched to see the reaction as a troop of foraging monkeys approached. The monkeys ignored it. The experiment was repeated, but this time by creating a trail in the grass resembling that of a python. Again they were unimpressed. The scientists concluded that the monkeys were blind to secondary visual clues; they were, in fact, poor naturalists.

The test did, however, point out a fundamental difference between monkeys and humans. People are naturally curious about everything in their environment, whether it is of direct relevance to their survival or not. Monkeys, on the other hand, are interested only in things or events that have immediate practical value. Vervets in the Cameroon, for example, were played recordings of east African hippos and the alarm calls of black-winged stilts. They disregarded the hippo calls, even though they were unusual and out of context, but responded to the stilt even though they had never met one before. Likewise, east African vervets ignored the lowing of migrating wildebeest but became very agitated by the lowing of domestic cattle: cattle are usually accompanied by people, and vervets know that although cattle are harmless, people are not.

Scientists have been establishing the first few entries in the English-vervet dictionary, featuring a limited vervet vocabulary of word-like sounds, or protowords. Vervets have found a niche in which they are able to find enough food and live in comparative safety, and their chances of survival have been enhanced further by their ability to use protowords that not only warn of specific dangers but also trigger an immediate action in order to avoid being caught. They are not alone in this behaviour.

ALARM CALLS FOR SQUIRRELS

Belding's ground squirrels, living in the Sierra Nevada Mountains of California, also look out for their relatives. Like the vervets, they have specific alarm calls for aerial and ground predators. Attacks from the sky trigger a continuous high-pitched whistle, while terrestrial predators elicit a lower, segmented call. The calls are not given in response to any threat, however, for ground squirrels are discriminating rodents. They not only distinguish between harmless and dangerous animals, but they also recognise when potential predators do not pose an immediate threat.

Ground squirrels are cautious about hawks, falcons, harriers, magpies and egrets, but are less interested in pelicans, which are not predatory. Harriers flying directly over the burrow are considered dangerous and the squirrels give the alarm call, whereas those migrating south, for example, on the other side of a nearby river, are seen as less of a threat and are ignored. Similarly, egrets in the air are less likely to attack than those approaching on the ground.

Dogs, coyotes, minks and badgers like to eat squirrels, as do rattlesnakes and long-tailed weasels. If a squirrel spots one of these predators approaching, it stands on its hind legs, a form of behaviour known as 'posting', calls loudly and then escapes rapidly into its burrow.

Some predators, however, are quite capable of pursuing a squirrel down its burrow, so different predators trigger specific escape procedures: if dogs or coyotes are out hunting, the ground squirrel's alarm call seems to indicate 'dive down any burrow', since these animals are too large to follow them underground; but if badgers or ferrets approach, the message changes to 'dive down a burrow with a back door'.

Many birds also have specific alarm calls. The robin in an urban garden, for example, is often the first bird to spot the neighbourhood cat, to which it gives a clearly audible 'tick-tick' alarm call. Robins and other garden birds are able to fly away from a cat, so a loud, locatable alarm is perfectly satisfactory. But a crow or a sparrowhawk is less easy to escape from, so the robin gives a wispy, high-pitched call that the predator finds hard to locate. The caller is able to

WHO IS IT? *Belding's ground squirrels in California's Sierra Nevada Mountains have distinct alarm calls for different predators.*

VENTRILOQUISTS — CALLS THAT CANNOT BE TRACED

When danger threatens an animal, particularly one that lives in a group, it is faced with a dilemma: does it raise the alarm and thereby draw attention to itself, putting itself at considerable risk, or does it keep quiet and risk its relatives being caught? Since many pairs of alert eyes are more likely to spot a predator, social animals tend to rely on their fellow group-members for a warning. This is one reason why fish swim in shoals, antelope wander in herds and birds fly in flocks. For the system to work, group animals have to play their part in detecting predators and sounding the alarm, but some animals have found a way in which to minimise the danger to themselves.

For a predator to locate the source of a sound, the sound must be detectably discontinuous – that is, there is a slight delay between these stops and starts reaching the predator's right and left ears, which tells it in which direction to attack. Some birds have developed alarm calls that minimise these clues. They do this with high-pitched calls that fade in gradually, reach a climax and then slowly fade out, at a wavelength shorter than the distance between their ears.

In North America, the black-capped chickadee has one of these nonlocatable alarm calls. When a predator approaches a flock, the birds emit their alarm calls, known as 'high zees', at 8 kHz, fading in and out gradually, and attenuating rapidly in the environment. They are just loud enough to travel to other members in the flock but no farther. Unlike the calls of stonechats or robins, these calls are not thought to be aimed at offspring or the rest of the flock: youngsters, for instance, often disperse to other flocks many miles away. Rather, the secret lies in the long-term monogamous mating system. Mated

pairs of chickadees stay close together in the same flock, and alarm calls are directed at the mate and no one else, protecting it from predation. In this way, a pair of successful breeding birds ensure

WHERE IS IT? *Predators find it hard to locate the black-capped chickadee's alarm call.*

that they survive together until the next breeding season.

---

give an alarm that other birds seem to hear, without drawing too much attention to itself.

Bird alarms fall into three categories: those that travel short distances and are hard to pinpoint, like the hawk alarm of the robin; clear shrieks of despair like the alarm call of the redshank, which is dubbed the sentinel of the salt marsh because it warns all the other waders of approaching danger; and hard-edged rattling calls, like those of the jay and the thrush, which invite the neighbours to join in mobbing behaviour in order to scare off a predator.

One bird, the European stonechat, has two types of call. Throughout the breeding season the stonechat has a characteristic alarm call with two distinct components. One note is a thin, short, whistled sound – a 'whit' – while the second is a more raucous 'chat' sound that is rather like the noise of two stones being

ROBIN TALK *The robin has a 'thin' alarm call to warn off hawks but greets the local cat with a loud 'tick-tick' call.*

banged together. The stonechat uses the two notes in different ways, depending on the type of predator.

Stonechats face two types of hazard: birds of prey that attack from the air, taking not only the adult birds but their chicks as well; and ground predators, which are a threat only to the nestlings. A sparrowhawk will provoke a whit call, whereas dogs and people are greeted by whit and chat calls mixed together. The wispy whit call alerts the nestlings to stop begging and to lie still, lest they attract the predator's attention.

The combination of whit and chat calls, delivered in a frantic barrage of sound, are accompanied by a visual display of wing-flicking that exposes the white flashes on the stonechat's conspicuous wing coverts. The whit calls again warn the chicks to remain still and silent, while the chat calls together with the erratic flying display lure the predator away from the site of the nest.

THE DECEIVERS' ART

Social animals, from apes to insects, can be quite as cunning as humans. To gain an advantage over the rest of their group, some individuals use fraud or artful trickery – in other words, they cheat.

Some animals deceive to stay alive. When a lion approaches an ostrich that is incubating eggs or guarding nestlings, the adult bird will run some distance from the nest and flop down as if injured. It then staggers around with one wing hanging down in what is described as a 'broken-wing display'. The lion, intrigued no doubt by the behaviour and anticipating an easy meal, gives chase. Imagine its surprise when the ostrich leaps up and makes off across the savannah at high speed, propelled by its enormously powerful legs. The eggs or nestlings are safe, and when the lion has successfully been lured some distance away, the parent bird can return to the nest and continue incubating or brooding.

Is the bird behaving intelligently? Is it simply encouraging the lion to run away from the nest, or does it really want the lion to believe it is injured – a very complex piece of reasoning? There is, alas, no answer, for

DISTRACTION *The North American killdeer performs a 'broken-wing' distraction display.*

science has yet to devise a test for such behaviour, but there are indications from other species that the behaviour of the parent bird is sometimes dependent on the nature and behaviour of the predator.

The killdeer plover has a broken-wing distraction display. If it is approached by a dog or a person, it flaps its wings erratically and spreads its tail, looking to all the world like a very sick bird. This tends to attract a predator's attention and lures the animal away from its nest on the ground. If a domestic cow approaches, however, the behaviour is different. The cow might trample the eggs, but otherwise is not dangerous. In this case, the plover remains close to the nest site, flying continuously at the cow's face until it turns and heads off in another direction.

Birds apart, the great deceivers in the animal world are the apes and monkeys, who seem to excel at reading each other's minds and manipulating each other's behaviour. Those same vervet monkeys that developed alarm calls for specific predators, have also applied their linguistic skills to skulduggery.

Consider this occasion, observed in Kenya. A nervous male vervet spotted an unknown vervet watching his troop from a short distance away. The resident's troop was feeding below a stand of acacia trees, and the intruder had to cross a piece of open grassland between one stand of trees and another in order to reach them. The resident male was nervous that the new arrival might pick a fight and displace him as the troop's dominant male. So, as the stranger set out across the open ground, he gave the leopard alarm call and the intruding male raced back to the nearest tree and climbed to the topmost branches. Throughout the day, the stranger tried to brave the open ground and cross the gap, but each time it started to approach the troop the resident male gave the alarm call and it retreated.

The resident vervets remained in their acacia grove overnight, while the intruder stayed in his. The next morning, however, the resident male destroyed his chances by giving the game away. It delivered the

leopard alarm call continuously while it walked nonchalantly in the open. The stranger realised immediately that there were no leopards about and simply crossed the gap and joined the troop. The resident male was able to manipulate the other's behaviour, but not entirely. He had failed to work out the other's point of view and had not realised that the stranger might see through the deception.

ARTFUL CHIMPANZEES

Gaining food by deception is sometimes worth a try. Chimpanzees are past masters at this art, and the propensity starts at an early age. The chimpanzee researcher Jane

BRAVE ATTEMPT *Blacksmith plovers try to lure a young Cape buffalo away from their nest site.*

Goodall tells many stories of her study group in the Gombe National Park in Tanzania. There was, for instance, an occasion when a chimpanzee infant was being weaned and its mother refused it milk. The devious youngster craftily groomed its mother around her nipple and took a surreptitious slurp when she was looking the other way.

On another occasion, a dominant male was eating a piece of meat. One of the younger males sidled up and started to groom him. After a bout of intensive grooming, however, the subordinate began to groom with one hand only, while the other was inching its way closer and closer to a scrap of meat. Having procured the morsel, the subordinate stopped grooming the dominant male and then strolled off to enjoy his ill-gotten gains.

Another young male spotted a banana that had been placed in a tree by the research team. Unfortunately, it was directly above the same dominant male and if the youngster had gone to fetch it, the older chimpanzee would certainly have taken it. So, the young chimp waited tight-lipped, trying not to draw attention to the spot. The moment the dominant male left, the youngster quickly ran in, climbed the tree and grabbed the fruit.

Chimpanzees have been studied even more closely in captivity. At Arnhem Zoo in the Netherlands, a group of chimpanzees live in a large enclosure. One day they were shown a box full of grapefruits and then locked in their sleeping quarters. The scientist studying them took the grapefruits and buried them in the sand in such a way that small patches of yellow were just

visible. The group was then shown the empty box and allowed to enter the enclosure: the chimpanzees therefore knew that somewhere there was a treasure trove of delicious fruit and rushed madly about searching for it.

They even ran over the spot where the grapefruits had been buried, but none of them stopped, including one young male whom the researchers called Dandy. As it

SORTING OUT BABY

Chimpanzee mothers, like human ones, can become exasperated with the unrelenting demands of their offspring. They even resort to subterfuge, diverting a little one's attention from nursing by starting to groom it or by playing games. A whimpering infant may be greeted with hoots of laughter and a game that ends up with the infant being towed along the ground by the harassed parent. Youngsters apparently enjoy being bumped along the ground and eventually jump up and run off to play elsewhere, their need for milk forgotten.

happened, Dandy had, in fact, spotted the grapefruits but did not pass the information on to his fellows. He ignored the fruit, rushing about with the others, pretending to search. But when the time came for the

troop to return to its quarters, Dandy remained behind and dug up the fruit.

In a laboratory study in the USA, chimpanzees have shown just how devious they can be. In one experiment, a chimpanzee watched as food was hidden in one of two containers. After a while, one of the human trainers entered the cage, and if the chimpanzee showed him where the food was hidden, the trainer shared the spoils with it. On other occasions, a second trainer entered the cage, but kept all the food to himself, even if the chimpanzee had located it correctly.

When this had happened several times, the chimpanzee became less cooperative with the second trainer. At first it refused to show the second trainer where the food was hidden, and then went further still in its peeved disappointment: it pointed to the wrong container.

However, such a study poses more questions than it answers. For example, the chimpanzee was not confused when the second trainer failed to look in the other container; after all, there were only two containers and the food was in one of them. The chimp either did not understand the relationship between the trainer's know-how and his actions, or he thought the man was stupid.

INSECT FRAUDS

Deceit and a little cunning sometimes gain an individual animal an advantage at the expense of its fellows. What is often not clear, however, is whether the cheating is intentional behaviour or merely triggered automatically by events. Male scorpion flies, for example, have the habit of presenting a gift-wrapped package of prey to a female before mating with her, but some

ENTERPRISING BABOONS

In a study of baboons in South Africa's Drakensberg Mountains, two Scottish researchers – Dick Byrne and Andrew Whiten – noticed that youngsters were fooling the other members of the troop into thinking something was wrong in order to benefit from the ensuing confusion.

One young baboon was observed watching an unrelated adult female dig for roots and tubers. The female was having some success – that is, until the youngster checked whether there were any other members of the troop about and then screamed loudly as if it was being attacked. Its mother appeared, saw the lone female and, assuming that she was the aggressor, chased her away. When the two females disappeared, the young baboon walked over to the digging site and ate his fill.

On another occasion, an older

male baboon bully tried another trick in order to get out of trouble. He was beating up a juvenile when the youngster's family and friends came running to its aid. Sensing that he was about to be punished, the baboon stood on his hind legs and stared intently at the horizon. The others stopped dead in their

OLIVE LUCK *Olive baboons cry 'wolf' and get away with it.*

tracks and did the same. Staring behaviour is the normal way in which members of the troop alert the others to approaching danger. The bully had avoided a beating through his deceitful behaviour.

above the ground. Whatever the species, fireflies find a mate of the correct species by matching flashes. Some, though, deliberately set out to break the code and gain an advantage.

Female fireflies of the genus *Photuris* not only signal to their own kind, but also mimic the signals of other species. A male *Photinus* firefly flying overhead spots a female giving the correct signal and drops down to court her; every time he gives his signal the *Photuris* female replies with the correct code. He is transfixed and homes in on her flashing light. But just as he reaches her, his expectation of mating is interrupted as she grabs and eats him. Her deception has gained her extra nutrients for her eggs.

When female fireflies are waiting for a prospective mate or laying eggs, they are vulnerable to predators, such as wolf spiders and ants. *Photinus* females, however, have a defence mechanism. Both females and males have poisonous steroids in their blood, known as lucibufagins (related to toad poisons and among the deadliest poisons known to science), making them unpleasant to eat. *Photuris* females do not have the poisons, but by eating *Photinus* males, they gain both a meal and the protective chemicals.

The behaviour of species, however, is modified by experience. In the parts of North America where this kind of deception takes place, male fireflies behave differently to their counterparts in other places. The males now give a quick flash and drop to the ground rather than flying directly to the female, and one species has given up flashing altogether.

ABSENT PARENTS

Cuckoos are cheats. They have given up all responsibility for rearing their own young and instead deceive other, hard-working parents into accepting their eggs and bringing up their chicks. The European

males imitate females, grab the gift and make off with it in order to present it to a female themselves.

Ants have two olfactory (smell) signals – one that provokes an attack on a predator and one that encourages them all to retreat. However, some species of slave-making ants have discovered that they can manipulate the behaviour of others by using one of the signals out of its usual context. They enter the nest of a species that they wish to enslave and spray the 'run away' odour. The nest empties and the

FIRE FOOLS *Female fireflies trick males of another species into thinking that they are ready to mate, and then eat them.*

invaders walk in unchallenged to snatch the larvae and pupae, which they take back to their own nest and breed as slaves.

A similar form of deceit is demonstrated by the *femme fatale* of the insect world – the firefly. The channel of communication exploited in this case is not smell but vision. More than 3000 years ago, Chinese poets wrote lyrically about the light of the firefly, but little did they know of the treachery contained in the tiny flashing lights.

Each firefly has its own Morse code. Male *Photinus pyralis*, for example, flit on an undulating course just 20 in (50 cm) above the ground, dropping down every 5.8 seconds and giving a half-second flash; any female within 7 ft (2 m) waits for two seconds and then flashes back. *P. consanguineus* have a different flash pattern – two short flashes, two seconds apart, repeated every five seconds. *P. consimilis* males have slow flashes, delivered three at a time while the insect is between 10 ft (3 m) and 13 ft (4 m)

CUCKOO'S NEST *The female European cuckoo tosses out a reed warbler's egg (top) and replaces it with one of its own. The young cuckoo (bottom) pushes out the remaining warbler eggs.*

OUTSIZED CHILDREN *The cuckoo chick grows so large it dwarfs its foster parents.*

cuckoo is a past master of this behaviour.

Common cuckoo parents do not form a lasting relationship, but before they go their separate ways they must cooperate in order to cheat their targeted host. After mating, the female cuckoo looks for suitable host nests within her territory and then the pair get to work. Sometime during the afternoon – the timing is crucial – the male cuckoo creates a diversionary fuss in order to persuade the chosen host bird to leave its nest and give chase. The female, meanwhile, hides nearby, waiting for the potential foster parent's attention to be drawn elsewhere. When she sees that the coast is clear, she visits the target nest. She removes one of the host's eggs, so that her egg will be less likely to be noticed, and lays one of her own in its place. Then she makes off before the host returns. The

whole episode takes just 10 to 15 seconds and culminates in the female cuckoo eating the stolen egg. The pair then visit other nests in the female's territory, the male repeating his performance until the female cuckoo has laid all her eggs in different host nests.

If the cuckoo lays its eggs in the host nests in the morning, they are rejected. If the host bird's eggs are well advanced, then again, the intruder's will be thrown out. The cuckoo's success in deceiving other birds into accepting its eggs does not lie just in its exact sense of timing, however, but also in its choice of host.

In Britain, cuckoos target the nests of four main species, the choice depending on local conditions: on moorland, the nests of meadow pipits are parasitised; in

marshland, reed warblers are selected; around farms and in woodlands, dunnocks are targeted; and in open habitats, pied wagtails provide foster parents. Individual cuckoos specialise in one type of host, the female depositing eggs that mimic the colour of the host's eggs in order to minimise the chances of detection.

The exception to this is the dunnock cuckoo, which lays pale, spotted eggs although the host has blue eggs. The reason is thought to be that cuckoos have only recently begun to use dunnocks as hosts and the dunnocks have not had a chance to catch up with the deception.

IN PLACE
OF SPEECH

UNDER THE ICE *Walruses use chirps and burps to communicate with one another.*

ALL ANIMALS COMMUNICATE, AND FOR THEIR SAKE NATURE HAS TAKEN ADVANTAGE OF ALMOST EVERY CHANNEL OF COMMUNICATION IMAGINABLE. THERE ARE VISUAL, AUDITORY AND OLFACTORY SIGNALS — EXPLOITING, RESPECTIVELY, THE FACULTIES OF SIGHT, HEARING AND SMELL. MANY OF THESE SIGNALS ARE BEYOND HUMAN PERCEPTION — VERY HIGH AND LOW-FREQUENCY SOUNDS, INFRARED AND ULTRAVIOLET LIGHT AND SO ON. AND THEN THERE ARE SIGNALS CONVEYED BY VIBRATION, AND BY TOUCH. A FEW SPECIES OF FISH EVEN USE WEAK ELECTRIC FIELDS TO CONVEY THEIR MESSAGES TO ONE ANOTHER, AND SIMPLE SINGLE-CELLED ANIMALS CAN COMMUNICATE WITH OTHERS OF THEIR KIND — BY USING CHEMICALS.

FOOD DANCE *Honeybees dance to tell others where food is.*

ANIMAL TALK

Animals need to communicate with others of their kind. Mothers scold or reassure babies; strutting males warn off any rivals, and consenting adults check on sex, age and suitability before mating.

Animals rarely draw attention to themselves, since it could be dangerous. Whether predator or prey, most prefer to remain hidden, blending into the background, and ready to pounce or run as the case may be. So an animal that advertises its presence with a loud call, a brightly coloured flash of plumage or a detectable odour must be doing so for good reason. This kind of behaviour –

communication – must be important enough for the animal to take the risk.

In the main, animals need to communicate with others of the same species. The reasons can be various: to ward off rivals; to entice partners; to warn of danger; to demarcate a living space; or simply to identify gender, species or state of mind. Some animals utter sounds that clearly identify them as individuals. Adult penguins and their chicks can find each other, even in a noisy colony, by the sounds they make. And primates, such as

THE VOICE OF THE KING *Each member of a king penguin colony has its own distinctive voice.*

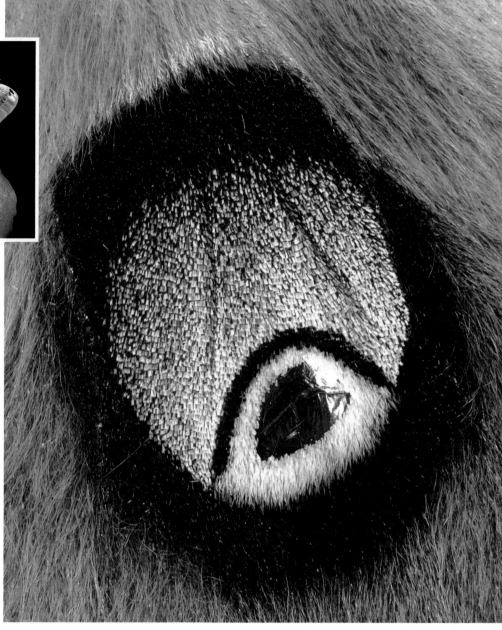

FALSE EYES *Eyespots on the wings of the polyphemus moth frighten predators. The pattern (right) is made from hundreds of tiny, coloured scales.*

monkeys and apes living in groups, have voices that their fellows can distinguish and associate with particular individuals.

Sometimes animals wish to 'speak' with others of a different species: the black-and-white stripes of a skunk, for instance, warn a mountain lion to keep its distance or it will be squirted with a foul-smelling spray. The orange-and-black hues of monarch butterflies warn birds not to eat them because they taste bad. The animal receiving the message may belong to the same species as the sender or to a different one – in either case, it is always the sender that is manipulating the receiver's behaviour.

LANGUAGE THAT DECEIVES

Such messages tend to be accurate and useful to the receiver, but not always. The viceroy butterfly from North America, for example, tells downright lies. It mimics the colours of the monarch butterfly and dupes birds into believing that it tastes horrible. In fact, it is as juicy and palatable as any other nonpoisonous butterfly. Likewise the hawk moth fools bird predators into supposing it is more ferocious than it really is: when under attack, it unfolds its wings and reveals two huge eyespots that resemble the eyes of a creature much bigger than a humble moth.

Animal talk, with the exception of certain 'words' uttered by monkeys and apes and the specific alarm calls given by birds and mammals, is generally rather imprecise. Unlike words in the human language, animal signals convey ill-defined messages, the equivalent of our smile, raised eyebrow or grunt of recognition.

They can be graded. The snarl of a wolf can convey mild irritability or downright displeasure depending on how forcefully it is delivered. The intensity of a signal and the frequency with which it is delivered may vary from one individual to another. Red deer stags, for example, roar at rivals in contests for the right to mate with a harem of hinds.

Deer are equipped with dangerous weapons on their heads and a fight could result in serious injuries to one or both of the contestants. By roaring, the stags assess each other's strengths and weaknesses, thus avoiding a real fight. A stag that roars at ten roars per minute will win a roaring contest against one that can only manage five per minute. The loser backs down before the dispute escalates into violence. The rate of roaring is an indication of a stag's fitness and gives a reliable assessment of how an animal might perform in a fight.

The quality of a call may also be significant. Female toads, for example, seem to prefer big male toads with deep voices; as a result, the deeper a male's voice the more chance he has of being picked as a mate. A deep voice is equated with a large, successful toad. He is a survivor and will, therefore, probably pass this characteristic on to his offspring. Such a toad is bound to be in demand, and the female's only method of assessing his suitability is by the pitch of his voice.

Some toads cheat, however. Male North American Fowler's toads have found a way to deepen their voices. Changes in temperature can vary the pitch of the call and so by sitting in the cooler parts of ponds, relatively small toads are able to compete with their larger rivals.

SINGING WHALES

Toad sounds are stereotyped – that is, they are fairly constant from one occasion to the next and from one individual to another. They are repeated with little variation and with no shades of meaning – a common feature of many animal signals. The reason for this is that an individual is not the only creature sending signals. There is a whole cacophony of sounds, smells and sights being transmitted at any one time. An individual's signal must therefore be distinct and stand out clearly from the background 'noise'. One way of doing this is to repeat a constant signal

BARED TEETH *Showing or not showing teeth speaks louder than words in wolf language.*

over and over again. Amorous humpback whales do this.

Humpbacks spend their summers in polar seas feeding on krill (tiny marine crustaceans) and small fish, and their winters in tropical waters breeding. The male whales space themselves out in the ocean in enormous traditional breeding sites known as 'leks', such as Silver Bank in the West Indies or close to the Hawaiian islands in the Pacific. A lek is nature's 'singles bar' – a display arena where males of a species congregate to show off their prowess, and females visit to find the fittest partner. The most eligible males tend to occupy positions at the centre of the lek, putting on displays that signal to rivals that they should keep their distance and to females that they are ready, waiting and very desirable. Male humpbacks use sound to signal their position and availability.

It is likely that humpback whales were

responsible for many ancient maritime legends. When the Irish saint Brendan and his entourage set sail from Ireland across the North Atlantic in the 6th century AD in search of 'that paradise amid the waves of the sea', he chanced upon a mysterious island around which he could hear heavenly choirs singing hymns. The island was probably Bermuda and the singers were not humans but whales. The whales arrive there each autumn and have almost certainly been doing so for centuries, but their eerie and melancholy sounds were not recorded and identified by scientists until 1952.

The more remarkable part of the story, however, did not emerge until 1967, when US researchers Roger and Katherine Payne met acoustic engineer Frank Watlington and listened to his recordings of humpback whales. The Paynes were fascinated by the moans and whines and went in search of the creatures that had made them. They rented a sailing boat, in order to get close to the whales without frightening them, and cruised Bermudan waters, listening for the sounds of the whales.

One day they heard them, the sounds amplified through the bottom of the boat, and they noticed that some of the phrases sounded similar to those they had heard on Frank Watlington's tapes. They realised they were not listening to random sounds but to regular, repeating patterns: the humpbacks were singing true songs, like

SEXY VOICE *The deeper an American toad's call, the better chance it has of attracting a mate.*

those of birds. The songs, they later revealed, consist of long, complicated, repetitive sequences and each song lasts from five to more than thirty minutes.

The whale sings it over and over again without breaks, except for breathing, for many hours. Indeed, one male humpback, recorded in the West Indies by Howard and Lois Winn, sang for 22 hours. And it was still going strong when the Winns pulled up their hydrophone (underwater microphone) and headed for home. Arguably, humpback whales sing the longest songs for the greatest length of time of any known animal.

Analysis of the recorded sounds from Bermuda, Hawaii and elsewhere produced even more fascinating information. It turned out that all the whales in the same ocean sing the same song. Although the song is continually changing, all the whales keep up with the changes. Nobody knows who rings the changes – a dominant male, perhaps. But it is known that the whales in the northern Atlantic Ocean, including the West Indies, sing a different song from those around Hawaii in the north Pacific. And the songs sung by whales in the Northern Hemisphere differ from those in

the Southern Hemisphere. This is probably because the whales in each hemisphere are unlikely to meet as their migration cycles are out of step – the northern whales head to the Arctic when the southern whales are returning from the Antarctic.

All this suggests that the whales learn their songs, but when, where and from whom will be difficult to find out, since ocean research is expensive. Even so, researchers have already revealed some of

HUMPBACK HI-FI

Humpback whales make extraordinary sounds – but how they make them remains something of a mystery. They have no vocal cords, although they do have a larynx. One explanation put forward by whale experts is that they make the sounds by shunting air backwards and forwards among numerous air sacs and cavities inside their bodies. Certainly, the variety of noises – burps, moans, screams, belches, snores, grunts, knocks, chirps, whistles and clicks – is evidence of a remarkable sound-producing system.

the detail of how humpback-whale song evolves. They have discovered, for example, that whales, like people, are composers, except that they do not create new songs,

UNDERSEA SONGS *Bull humpback whales sing underwater songs that may last for several hours.*

but evolve minor variations. The changes are progressive and rapid, each component changing every two months. Taking a nursery rhyme analogy, in the first months an individual might be singing 'Mary, Mary, quite contrary, how does your garden grow?' and so on, while two months later one phrase would be modified so the rhyme became 'Mary, Mary, Mary, quite contrary, how does your garden grow?' During the course of a season, parts of a song may undergo rapid change – a drop in pitch, for example, or the addition of extra components – for several months and then be left alone while other parts of the song are modified. Newly created phrases are sung more rapidly than older phrases, and occasionally a new phrase is created by taking the first and last parts of older phrases and dropping the bit in the middle, much as the English language shortens 'I would' to 'I'd'.

Bull whales sing their songs mainly in the winter breeding grounds and occasionally during their migration – so what happens to their songs in between times? Whales, like elephants it seems, never forget. When they arrive at the breeding grounds each year the song is picked up again, unchanged from the end of the last season. Most of the changes take place during the breeding season in the tropics and not during the summer on the feeding grounds. Over a period of about eight years the entire song is renewed. Interestingly, if the recordings of humpback whales are speeded up, the whales sound just like birds.

HOW BIRDS LEARN THEIR SONGS

Birdsong is probably the most studied topic in animal communication. Unlike whales, birds are easy to see and hear; they can be kept in captivity, and scientists are able to work out with greater ease how they acquire and use their songs.

Birds learn their songs during a 'sensitive' period, typically when the bird is young. The male white-crowned sparrow of North America, for instance, learns his relatively simple song when he is between 10 and 50 days old, before he leaves the immediate area of his parental nest at two months old.

He does not start to sing properly, however, until several months later during his first spring. When he does start to sing he will generate an imitation of his local dialect. He learns not from his father, as one would expect, but probably from the neighbours. His song, though, is not an exact replica of his neighbours' songs. A bird will pick and choose song elements learned in its infancy and invent new portions of song as well.

Between the period of learning and the development of the mature song comes a practice period that is of great interest to scientists. This is when the song changes in identifiable stages – through 'subsong' to 'plastic song' and finally to adult song. Subsong is rather like the babbling of a human baby before it begins to talk, and plastic song is a kind of 'vocal play' when a bird experiments with the sounds it learns and the sounds it invents.

North American swamp sparrows, like their white-crowned relatives, learn songs when very young (during their first 60-70 days of life). But they do not start to experiment with what they have learned until 230-250 days. They

THE DANCE OF THE HONEYBEE

Language is considered to be a peculiarly human phenomenon. But there is another creature that communicates in an almost human way: the honeybee. Its remarkable skills of communication were revealed by Austrian zoologist Karl von Frisch in 1946. He discovered that honeybees talk to each other in an unusual code, by 'dancing'.

A scout worker bee returns to the colony with information about a rich source of pollen and nectar. Entering the hive, she is 'frisked' by the guards, who ensure she has the right smell. Inside, she behaves in a strange way. She runs about attracting the attention of other workers and they gather round her, pummelling her with their antennae. She then performs her dance. If the food is located nearby, the dance is simple. The worker performs a 'round dance', moving in a circular pattern, first one way, then the other, across the vertical surface of the comb. The vigour of the dance indicates the richness of the food source.

If the food is some distance away, the dance is more complicated. The scout bee moves across the comb but this time at a particular angle, waggling her abdomen as she goes. At the end of the straight part of the dance she stops waggling and circles to the right, back to her starting point. Then she moves across the comb once more, this time circling back to the left to the starting point.

The dance, known as the 'waggle' dance, is repeated again and again until enough recruits have received the message.

The important part of the dance is the 'waggle' sequence. The angle between a vertical line and the path of the worker bee equals the angle between the position of the Sun and the source of food. The length of the straight part of the dance and the number of waggles communicates the distance to the food, and the intensity of the dance indicates the richness of the food site. The entire dance is accompanied by buzzing, which is picked up by the legs and antennae of the other workers. This is also thought to help give information about distance and quality.

NEAR AND FAR *The 'round' dance (left) and 'waggle' dance (middle and right) indicate the position of the food source.*

SUN BEARINGS *The pattern of the bee's dance is related to the position of the Sun.*

UPRIGHT, DOWNRIGHT *The bees dance on the vertical comb to pass on the horizontal coordinates of the food source.*

and consonants that make up words. By breaking the songs down into these song syllables, the male bird is able to recombine them later when he sings in earnest.

In this way he retains the local sound but can place his own mark on the final version. He keeps some sound syllables as they were but modifies others, transforming them until they are further and further away from the original song syllable.

In the simple, 12-syllable song of the swamp sparrow, five or six syllables are straight copies of original syllables, one or two are improvised variations, and five or six are inventions. These invented and improvised syllables tend to be more complex than the straight copies, and it has led scientists to conclude that songbirds have a capacity for a truly creative process.

So far, scientists studying bird behaviour have focused on the vocal play of birds with relatively simple songs. An exciting degree of inventiveness remains to be discovered in the songs of the various members of the thrush family (including the nightingale), mockingbirds and the virtuoso of the bird world – the brown thrasher of North America. This has one of the most complex songs of any bird and can, at one point in its song, sing four sounds at once. How it does so, nobody knows.

BAY DIALECTS *The song pattern of the male white-crowned sparrow varies in different parts of San Francisco's Bay area.*

① Marin

② Berkeley

③ Sunset Beach

commit the songs to memory, without rehearsal, storing them for the best part of the summer, autumn and winter before they produce anything resembling the original – a quite extraordinary feat.

BIRDSONG REPERTOIRE

Not all birds learn songs during the first few weeks of life. In Europe, the song of a male great tit shares the greatest number of song elements with those of his neighbours in the year in which he set up his first territory. But he also shares song elements with birds that lived near the nest site where he hatched and fledged, indicating two song-learning periods – one in the nest and another after dispersal. North American red-winged blackbirds continue to learn new songs throughout their life, and the domestic form of the canary discards large portions of its old song in favour of new phrases each year.

Song learning is not confined to male songbirds. Females do not generally sing, but they still learn songs. Inbreeding has to be avoided for it might result in the propagation of 'bad genes', such as those that make an individual susceptible to disease. To avoid this, a female songbird avoids mating with a male that sings a song like her father's. But nor is she attracted to a male singing a song that is too different from her father's. A genetically distant male may also be an inappropriate mate, for he might have become adapted to different environmental conditions. The female therefore listens for males singing the songs in the dialect of her local population.

Whether male or female, birds are thought to commit their songs to memory in segments. A bird is able to break its song into phonetic units, known as 'phonemes', which are the equivalent of human syllables, consisting of different packages of vowels

BEYOND HUMAN HEARING

An animal may send signals in very high or very low-frequency sound – ultrasounds or infrasounds. They are inaudible to humans, but can be detected and analysed by sophisticated listening equipment.

Elephants are understandably wary of human beings, as the Masai people of East Africa have long noticed. For centuries, their herdsmen observed that any elephants they disturbed while watching their cattle were somehow able to mobilise all the other elephants in the area. Even animals some distance away would abandon what they were doing – dust-bathing, sleeping, feeding or drinking – and head away from the danger area.

They could hear no loud trumpetings or other unusual noises, but the elephants would move away, as if by magic. The Masai thought that the enormous animals – the largest of all land animals – possessed a mysterious channel of communication, and recent research has proved that they were right. Elephants really do have a hidden means of talking to each other – hidden, that is, from people.

The elephant's secret wavelength is nothing as exotic as mental telepathy or extrasensory perception. Rather, they 'rumble' to each other at sound frequencies well below the spectrum of human hearing. The sounds are known as 'infrasounds' and generally fall below 20 Hz. Healthy humans with good hearing can detect sounds between 20 and 2000 Hz. Above and below we hear nothing at all. Even at 30 Hz the sounds must be intense for us to hear them. Elephants communicate at even lower wavelengths.

ELEPHANT SONGS AND ORGAN PIPES

The discovery was made by Katherine Payne – the same scientist who unravelled the secrets of the songs of humpback whales – while she was visiting Portland Zoo in the USA. She stood in front of three Asian elephants with their calves and

AT THE WATER HOLE *With a single infrasonic grunt, the matriarch elephant will bring the bathing session to a halt and the group will move off.*

was aware of a throbbing feeling going through her body. It was the same sensation she had felt when she was a girl standing next to the biggest and deepest organ pipe in church. Perhaps the elephants were causing the vibrations just as the organ pipes had done. She decided to investigate and so returned to the zoo to record the elephants.

During the recording sessions she noticed that the vibrations she felt were accompanied by a fluttering movement of the skin on the elephants' foreheads. Most of the sounds they recorded, or so they thought at the time, were just audible to the human ear, but unknowingly they had recorded other sounds too. In the laboratory, where the sounds were converted into visual print-outs, the research team discovered that they had recorded sounds they could not hear. In fact, there were three times as many calls as they thought they had recorded, and they were at frequencies in a range between 14 and 24 Hz. The researchers then speeded up the recorded tapes slightly, which raised the pitch of the calls, and in doing so they became the first people to hear the secret voice of the elephant.

Infrasounds can travel long distances. An elephant's calls are thought to travel 12 miles (20 km) or more – an ability that would benefit creatures living in herds spread over a wide area. It is particularly important during courtship and mating. Elephant herds are made up mainly of females and youngsters, and are led by an elderly matriarch. Adult males live solitary lives. They wander wide and free, crisscrossing the home ranges of several female herds before finding a female on heat.

RUMBLE CALLS *African elephants use low-frequency 'rumbles' to communicate over long distances.*

In fact, the chances of finding a receptive female are very small. A pregnant cow has a gestation period of two years, and a mother nursing her offspring does so for a further two years or more. A female is only ready to mate for a few days every five years, so she cannot leave things to chance. She tips the odds in her favour with the help of infrasound. A receptive female calls out for a passing bull using a pattern of very low-frequency sounds. She makes them for about 30 minutes, and they are always presented in the same sequence. This kind of repeated pattern is usually known as a 'song' – until now the province of birds and humpback whales – and so, it seems, female elephants 'sing' for a partner.

The bulls arrive from far and wide, and they, too, are now grumbling excitedly with

JUMBO FRUSTRATION

In a study in Kenya, a loudspeaker on a van played recordings of a female elephant's sexual 'rumbles'. The researchers could not hear the low-frequency sounds but a passing bull could. He stopped, turned towards the sound and set off at high speed. The scientists were alarmed to see a sexually active elephant heading straight towards them and switched off the recording, expecting the experiment to end in chaos. The ardent suitor, however, charged straight past, searching vainly for the 'lover' who had been proclaiming her availability.

the so-called 'musth rumble'. When ready to mate, bulls are said to be in 'musth': that is, they have high levels of testosterone (the male sex hormone) circulating in their blood and they become very aggressive. If several bulls arrive in the area at the same time, and they are evenly matched for size and strength, they will fight to establish which of them has the right to mate with the receptive female.

On reaching the female herd, however, the winner calms down somewhat. A bull's rumbling decreases as the receptive female rumbles back at him. She then sings her 'loud song' and they mate. Then the female gives a 'post-copulatory rumble' that causes the rest of her herd to become very agitated. They rumble, trumpet and defecate in what researchers have called the 'mating pandemonium'.

But not all low-frequency elephant calls are related to mating. There are many everyday calls, such as greeting rumbles and contact rumbles. And if the herd is eating, drinking or mud-wallowing, the matriarch will give the 'let's go' rumble when it is time to leave. A baby elephant will tell its mother that it wants some milk with a 'suckle protest', and if it is in danger it gives a loud scream and the rest of the herd come running, each elephant giving its rendition of one of the loudest infrasonic rumbles known.

MYSTERY SOUNDS FROM UNDER THE SEA

An even louder low-frequency call can be heard in the world's oceans. It consists of pulses of sound with a frequency close to 20 Hz. With a bandwidth of only 3 Hz, it is

so loud that scientists once thought that it could not possibly come from anything living. It was a mystery.

When scientists recorded the 20 Hz signal, they noticed that each train of pulses, lasting about 15 minutes each, was separated by $2^{1}/_{2}$ minutes of silence. The rhythm was reminiscent of the breathing cycle of a giant baleen whale. After that discovery, American researchers placed an enormous three-dimensional array of hydrophones on the seabed. These meant that they were able not only to record any sounds in the area, but also to pinpoint which animals were making them. They found that the 20 Hz signal was being

FINS AND GROANS *Fin whales keep in touch using a regular pattern of low-frequency groans.*

made by fin whales, the second largest and the fastest of the baleen whales.

But why, scientists wondered, would fin whales want to make such a loud, low-frequency call? Many other creatures, including the smaller relatives of the whales – killer whales and dolphins – use sound signals to keep in touch with other members of the group. But fin whales tend to travel in ones and twos.

Using the multiple hydrophone array, the scientists were able to watch and listen to a pair of fin whales that were swimming several miles apart. The first whale was heard to call for about three hours while heading south. The second whale, swimming on a parallel course, but 3 miles (5 km) to the east, then began to call. Immediately the first whale changed direction and headed towards the second whale. Was it responding to the second whale's call? Could it be that fin whales do not travel alone but as part of a

HI-FI COMMUNICATION *Spotted dolphins emit very high-frequency clicks and audible squeaks, burps and screams.*

large, widely scattered herd? Low-frequency sounds may be the means by which members of the group stay in touch. As yet, there is no answer, though there are some clues.

CLICK LANGUAGE

Although sperm whales are not much smaller than fin whales, they communicate not at the low-frequency end of the sound spectrum, but at the very high-frequency end. They use ultrasound. Sperm whales belong to a group of marine mammals known as the odontocetes, or 'toothed whales', which also includes dolphins, porpoises, killer whales, pilot whales, belugas, narwhals, beaked whales and river dolphins. All odontocetes communicate at these higher frequencies.

Sperm whales communicate by clicks, some of which are produced at such a speed that they seem to fuse into a creaking sound similar to that made by a rusty hinge. Each herd of whales has its own sound signature – a series of clicks uttered in a pattern and known as a 'coda' – that is peculiar to a particular group. The whales use their coda to identify members of the herd during roll calls, such as after a deep

HOW DOLPHINS SEE WITH SOUND

Dolphins produce their click sounds by shunting air backwards and forwards in the complicated plumbing system beneath their blowholes. The sounds then pass through the bulbous melon in the forehead, which acts like an acoustic lens, focusing them into a thin, pencil beam. They bounce off objects in the sea and the returning echoes are picked up by the teeth in the dolphin's bottom jaw. The sounds then pass along a fat-filled channel in the lower jaw to the ear.

Dolphins often produce their clicks so rapidly that to human ears the sounds appear to fuse together. A click-train may contain 700

SOUND GUN
The dolphin's sound beam can disable prey.

packages of sound per second, yet the dolphin is able to separate them in the brain, distinguishing individual echoes and decoding the information while interrogating a target. A dolphin is able to identify

a tangerine-sized object at 390 ft (120 m). It can tell if it is solid or hollow, made of aluminium or steel, and not only recognises whether it is dead or alive, but also whether it is friendly or aggressive.

WHALE SONG

Most whales communicate with sound. One of the noisiest is the beluga or white whale of the Arctic. Its huge repertoire of chirps and screams used to be heard through the wooden hulls of sailing ships, whose sailors called the whales 'sea canaries'. Their sounds travel well and whales on either side of a 4000-strong herd can communicate with each other. They are timid animals and when alarmed will dive as one and head for deep waters, their entire retreat coordinated by a chorus of extraordinary noises.

dive. The sperm whale herd, consisting of females and youngsters (the bulls accompany the herd only when breeding), dives together. As the whales descend, they fan

out to feed in the depths and then come together once more, to within 33 ft (10 m) of each other, at the surface. They locate and recognise each other by clicking.

The sounds can travel considerable distances. Ultrasound is not particularly good for transmitting messages over long distances under water, but sperm whales, being big animals with big sound-producing organs, 'shout' very loudly. Sperm whales several miles apart exchange information such as warnings and danger signals, and the sounds serve to rally the herd.

French aquanaut and film-maker Jacques-Yves Cousteau and his team once followed some sperm whales in the Indian Ocean and witnessed how devious they could be. They were following a harem of cows and juveniles that were accompanied by a dominant male 'schoolmaster'. At first they heard a variety of sounds in their hydrophones, but as they approached more closely they heard a very loud burst of clicks from the large

bull whale. The rest of the group fell silent. Then the bull sidled up to Cousteau's ship and spouted for all he was worth. He seemed to be deliberately making himself conspicuous, drawing the research team away. Meanwhile the harem made a silent exit in the opposite direction. The bull sperm whale had tried to fool the humans into following him, thereby saving his harem. There had also been a conversation of clicks and a degree of cooperation:

SIGNING OFF *Sperm whales have their own ultrasonic 'click signatures'.*

SENDING OUT SOUND *Flaps inside the sperm whale's snout direct and focus the sound.*

Resonators
The sounds resonate in hollow sacs at the front and back of the head.

Blowhole
Flaps in the blowhole shut tight.

Monkey's muzzle
Sounds are thought to originate in the *museau de singe* – literally, 'muzzle of the monkey'.

Spermaceti
The sounds are focused in the oil-filled spermaceti organ.

THE CLICKS OF THE SPERM WHALE

every individual in the herd seemed to know what it should be doing.

The clicks have a dual function. They are not only communication signals, but are also used for echolocation, or orientation. As the whales dive they produce clicks almost continuously. In the dark depths of the sea, whales are unlikely to see their prey, so they use sound. The click sounds are thought to be produced amongst the tubes and sacs in the head and then focused into a beam by the huge oil-filled spermaceti organ that occupies most of the gigantic forehead. The sound beam projects forward and bounces off obstacles such as fish or squid, in the water ahead. The returning echoes are detected by the whale, providing it with information about the nature, speed and direction of the prey. Occasionally, loud clicks are heard that resemble gunshots. It is thought that

BIG HEAD, BIG NOISE *The sperm whale's huge snout is a sound-producing centre.*

these are very high-intensity pulses that are used to debilitate or even kill the prey. Although nobody has actually seen a sperm whale dispatch its prey in this way, evidence seems to suggest that this is the most likely way it catches a meal.

This same killer beam may also have a less threatening role in social interactions. A whale may use the beam to interrogate an approaching whale, recognising both its 'acoustic silhouette' and its intention. An interesting property of ultrasound is that it can 'see' inside another's body. This ability to probe without causing damage is used by obstetricians to check the health of an unborn baby. Scientists speculate that one sperm whale may be able to assess another's mood by checking its heart rate. If it is agitated the heart rate will go up, whereas if it is calm the heart rate will be normal.

Because they are equipped with such a

sophisticated sound system and show such advanced behaviour, it is easy to believe that whales, and their smaller relatives the dolphins, possess some 'superintelligence'. They do have large brains – indeed, the sperm whale has the largest brain of any living animal – but it must be remembered that processing this acoustic information ties up enormous amounts of brain power. This probably leaves little room for intelligent behaviour on a par with humans'.

A few scientists have claimed that dolphins really are as intelligent as we are. Most famous amongst them was John Lilly, the inspiration for the book and film *The Day of the Dolphin*. Lilly moved on from human-brain research after he had seen the brain of a dolphin and was impressed by its size and complexity. He became involved with training dolphins and, among other things, taught them spoken English: one dolphin could say 'stop it' and 'bye-bye' and another could count up to ten.

But English is not the best way to reach the dolphin mind, though the creatures are remarkably quick mimics. In tests, dolphins have been known to make a sound even before the signal it was copying was finished. In one test a trainer gave dolphins a series of vowel and consonant sounds to mimic and the dolphins were accurate about 70 per cent of the time. The dolphins were appreciating some aspects of their tests, even if it was doubtful how much they understood the meaning.

There was, however, an occasion when Lilly was surprised. The astronomer Carl Sagan was visiting. One of the dolphins, called Elvar, swam over to the side of the tank and presented his underside for tickling. Sagan tickled him. Elvar moved away but returned for another bout, only this time he stopped in water that was a bit deeper. This happened several times, with Elvar resting in deeper water each time. Eventually, Sagan could not reach any farther without falling in and he stopped tickling. Elvar instantly raised himself out of the water, stood on his tail and, towering above the two men, clearly said: 'More.' Had the dolphin appreciated the meaning of 'more', or had it used the word because it gained the right response? Either way, both Sagan and Lilly were impressed.

CLICK LANGUAGE AND A GATHERING OF THE CLANS

Dolphins, killer whales (or orcas) and all the other toothed whales produce ultrasonic clicks. With the exception of sperm whales, these creatures probably use clicks for echolocation and have a separate vocabulary of audible burps, squawks and whistles for communication.

Orcas living near Vancouver, Canada, for example, have a large repertoire of clicks, whistles and pulsed calls. The clicks and whistles appear to function as echolocation signals and contact calls. The pulsed calls, of which there are about 12 distinct patterns, are heard when the pod (group) of orcas is spread out and foraging for food. They are stereotyped, each member of the pod producing the same calls, and all of the calls are repeated during a 30-minute period, whatever the pod's behaviour at the time. Each pod has its own dialect, which changes little for many years.

Several pods in the Vancouver area have similar dialects, indicating that they must be descended from a single ancestral pod that grew too big and broke up into smaller groups. Pods of orcas, like elephant herds, tend to be stable matriarchal groups. The pods which have similar dialects can be considered members of the same 'clan'. The existence of dialects and clans also indicates that killer-whale utterances must have been learned.

The dialects, however, are different from those of songbirds. Bird dialects are usually the result of geographical isolation, whereas orca dialects are specific to a group even in a localised area. Such dialects are rare in mammals. In fact, only killer whales and man are known to share this cultural transmission of dialects.

IN THE FAMILY *Killer whales have distinctive family calls in a variety of local dialects.*

SIGN LANGUAGE

Almost every external part of an animal's body can be used in communication. An animal may wave its limbs, nod its head, wag its tail, change its colour, bare its teeth, spread its wings or raise its hackles.

A scuba diver slowly approaches a grey reef shark over a coral reef in the Pacific. The shark would not normally attack; indeed, it would usually avoid humans. But the diver – a marine biologist studying aggressive behaviour in sharks – moves deliberately towards it, provoking it to attack him. At first the shark tries to shirk the confrontation, but as the diver draws nearer, it starts to behave strangely. It arches its back, drops its pectoral fins, lifts its snout and swims in a stiff and awkward fashion. The diver – protected by a chain-mail diving suit – presses on. Suddenly, the shark darts forward, slashes with an open mouth at the diver's arm, and then swims rapidly away.

There are more than 375 varieties of shark, and none is a great conversationalist. They do not produce sounds as many other fishes do. They do not have brightly coloured parts to the body with which to flash signals. And they do not leave long-lasting scent marks around their territories. Instead they 'talk' with their entire bodies. The unusual posture of the grey reef shark is a warning. The exaggerated swimming pattern says 'keep your distance or I'll attack', and if the signal is ignored it does just that – it attacks. It has communicated its intentions not with sound or scent but with body language.

In the wild, body language is important. A large great white shark, for instance, will show its displeasure when confronted by a shark of lesser size by shaking its head. Physical confrontation between two animals could result in one of the pair of rivals being injured or even killed. This risk is avoided by sending out the right signals – in this case visual signals. These messages become all the more important when large numbers of animals are in contact with one another. Visible social signals are important to maintain some kind of order. Most species of shark tend to be solitary creatures, but occasionally they come together in large numbers, mainly for courtship and mating, though sometimes just to rest in the safety of a school.

Hammerhead sharks in the eastern Pacific, for example, congregate at seamounts. These are underwater mountains, often the roots of ancient volcanoes, that do not reach the surface. At night the sharks hunt alone in the surrounding area but by day they arrive at these traditional meeting places and simply swim aimlessly up and down in formation – older sharks at the top and younger

BODY LANGUAGE *Like many sharks, nurse sharks 'speak' with body movements.*

ones at the bottom. Scientists who have watched them have noticed that during their daily promenade known as 'refuging behaviour' they make curious swimming movements. Every so often, a shark will shake its head, swim off to one side, turn through 360° in a corkscrew motion and butt the shark underneath or in front. What this form of body language is saying is not known for the moment, but clearly these strange swimming movements carry a message that is important for the cohesion of the group – perhaps establishing a hierarchy in which each shark knows its status and its place.

Sharks tend to be thought of as 'mindless' killing machines. In reality, they appear to be relatively intelligent and sophisticated animals, the product of 300 million years of evolution. Some sharks have large brains compared with their body size, although a greater part of their

brain power is thought to be dedicated to interpreting odours during hunting and feeding. In the laboratory, sharks have shown that they are also capable of learning tasks as quickly as birds and small mammals. Lemon sharks, which have been studied around the Bimini Atoll off the Florida coast, have learned to find their way around a maze as fast as rabbits.

In other tests it has been shown that sharks can modify their behaviour. Lemon sharks, which have featured in many experiments because they are common along the US Atlantic coast, have learned how to push a target with their snout and ring a bell at one place in their tank, and then swim to another to obtain their reward. And at a naval base on the California coast where seals, dolphins and small whales are trained to carry out military tasks, a pair of nurse sharks were trained to work rings over their heads just as dolphins do in

PINCER MOVEMENT *Fiddler crabs wave an enlarged pincer to attract a mate and ward off rivals.*

marine circuses. Dolphins are often considered to be superintelligent beings because of their ability to learn and perform such tasks. What, then, does this tell us about the intelligence of sharks? Unfortunately, shark research is expensive and an answer is a long way off, but the present findings hint at complex and meaningful messages being passed from one shark to another in the postures that researchers are only just learning to recognise.

SHAKE A LEG

'Languages' made up of postures and gestures are widespread in the animal kingdom. On the mud in a tropical mangrove swamp exposed at low tide, for instance, male fiddler crabs wave a single enormous, colourful pincer in the air. The crab is sending two quite different messages depending on who is watching. On the one hand, it is warning rival males to stay away; on the other hand, it is enticing females to come closer. Different species have distinct claw-waving patterns.

On the same mud flats male mudskippers raise their dorsal fins and stand on their tails in order to catch the eye of a passing female. In the forests of New Guinea and northern Queensland, normally noisy tree frogs are silenced by the overwhelming sounds of nearby waterfalls. They have given up calling and instead have taken to 'shaking a leg' to attract a mate. The cryptically coloured dark green frogs stretch their legs and flick out bright blue feet to advertise their presence.

Having fended off a rival and attracted a partner, some animals have to 'talk' themselves out of trouble. The male wolf spider has to appease his mate by waving his front legs and pedipalps (sensors attached to his head) in a particular and precise way. In one species, *Lycosa rabida*, the male flexes his forelegs and waves his pedipalps in a circular fashion. After several rotations, he raises one leg and extends it as if tapping.

At the same time the spider vibrates his abdomen and drums with his pedipalps. The female responds by waving her legs, but if the male deviates from the traditional sequence of signals she is liable to eat him.

Salticid spiders have even more dramatic displays, relying totally on vision for communication. The males are brightly coloured and usually display their coloured parts in performances that are peculiar to their species. They rock from side to side or jump sideways in front of the female and then wave their legs and pedipalps in particular patterns. The male *Saited barbites*, for example, waves his brightly coloured, hairy third pair of legs high in the air.

Many insects and spiders have a system of visual signalling and it is not confined to courtship and mating. Male wolf spiders, which often live in large groups, signal to one another to establish a hierarchy. There are leg-waving signals that indicate a dominant male, and submission postures used by nondominant males when attacked. Crickets and grasshoppers even communicate with species other than their own. They have leg-extending signals to deter predators. The giant weta of New Zealand,

STAY AWAY! *A North American katydid stages an unusual display to warn off a predator.*

for instance, stretches its enormous back legs high above its abdomen, while the North American katydid *Neobarrettia* opens its wings, raises its body on its second pair of legs, and holds its front pair of legs high above its head.

USE YOUR HEAD

Arms and legs are not the only parts of the body used for visual signalling. Iguanas, such as the Galápagos marine iguana and the rhinoceros iguana from the West Indies, nod their heads vigorously or do 'push-ups'. The male alligator lizard from Arizona moves its head from side to side. The movements are thought to be inherited rather than learned, for young lizards perform the displays as soon as they emerge from the egg. Tortoises also bob the head during courtship or in aggressive encounters with rivals.

When threatened by another male, the male collared lizard jumps up and down, its feet leaving the ground, while the chuckwalla gets its message across either by flattening or by inflating its body. The Gould's monitor of Australia stands erect on its hind limbs with its mouth open. Chameleons, despite an apparently peaceful way of life, can be extremely aggressive to adversaries and have a large repertoire of signals to show their intentions. Two opponents face each other, and inflate

SPIDER THREAT *A hairy baboon spider from South Africa performs its 'threat display'.*

their bodies to show off any colourful patches. They sway slightly from side to side and open their mouths wide to show the brightly coloured lining. As they have a powerful, sometimes lethal bite, this signalling can prevent injury or even death.

The male anole lizard of the West Indies has a brightly coloured, fan-shaped dewlap beneath the chin that can be retracted until it is almost invisible or expanded to a size often bigger than the animal's head. It flashes its conspicuous signal at rival males, females and predators. The male green anole, for instance, begins his courtship ritual by bobbing his head and expanding his dewlap. Then he approaches the female with a peculiar stiff-legged, strutting gait. Unfortunately for the male anole, snakes have learned to home in on the dewlap, and as a consequence, male lizards fall prey to snakes more often than females do.

Other lizards use visual displays to deter predators rather than attract mates. The frilled lizard of Australia has a large flap of skin around its head that it can expand suddenly like an umbrella. The Australian blue-tongued lizard signals by sticking out its enormous blue tongue. The bizarre display is thought to frighten predators such as birds.

BIRD RITUALS

Visual signals are generally short-range, intimate signals. Unless an animal is very large indeed, visual signals cannot be seen from far away. They cannot go round obstacles; they are also fleeting, and in their brevity contain less complex messages than other types of signals. They tend, then, to be associated with private conversations, such as those between a courting couple or two rival males jostling for the right to mate with a female. They often include dramatic changes in an animal's colour: the male bull's-eye fish, for example, is a silvery colour when it is intimidated but bright orange when aggressive.

But the most obvious colour changes – obvious, that is, to human eyes – are in the world of birds. In the breeding season many males moult their feathers and renew their plumage, thereby transforming themselves

from dull-coloured creatures that blend in with their backgrounds into very obvious, flamboyant beaus. They back up their colourful costumes with energetic dances and displays. The most extravagant are the displays performed by the birds of paradise in New Guinea and Australia.

The vividly coloured Count Raggi's bird of paradise demonstrates its prowess to visiting females in a special breeding ground or 'lek'. The male has a short, yellow-plumed crown on its head, a metallic green throat and, most spectacular of all, translucent orange plumes extending backwards over the tail.

Each year after the moult the birds develop even longer and more seductive feathers, and so the older the bird, the better its chance of winning a partner.

BLUE PERIL *The Australian blue-tongued lizard sticks out its gaudy tongue to frighten away predators.*

The performance begins at daylight when a single raucous call summons not only the relatively dowdy females, but also other males. The cocks stand little chance of success if they perform alone and so must compete in a group for the attention of the hens. By mid-morning the ensemble is ready and the first hen arrives. Suddenly pandemonium breaks out. The males call excitedly as they bend towards the hen, clapping their wings and casting their feathers towards her. As the tension rises, the calls turn into a high-pitched buzz. When a hen has selected a partner she sidles up to him and the performance changes from a frenzied commotion to a graceful ceremony. The chosen male now quietens and hangs upside-down from a tree branch to execute a stationary nuptial dance. He sways hypnotically from side to side and throws his amazing plumes over his head so that his richest, golden feathers dazzle his partner. Once the mating is over, the hen leaves as quickly as she arrived and brings up her brood alone.

Courtship, mating and other social interactions are curious in that the movements are meant to overcome a creature's natural tendency to avoid close contact with another member of the same species. Both are in competition for food and living space, and could easily do each other damage with sharp beaks or talons. So, courtship may show traces of behaviour associated with attacking and fleeing. The courtship flight of some eagles, for instance, often involves elaborate aerial dog-fights in which the birds grapple together, linking talons and dropping out of the sky. Because the powerful talons are neutralised when locked together, the birds are able to overcome their fear of each other. Similarly, a gull turns its head away from its partner, thus hiding its dangerous bill. Each bird reassures its partner that it is not going to attack.

FLASH A DEWLAP *A male green anole lizard in the Costa Rican rain forest attracts attention by flashing a brightly coloured dewlap.*

COURTLY LOVE *A male Raggianna bird of paradise (opposite) performs an elaborate display to impress a prospective partner.*

Throughout the rest of its everyday, normal life a bird may use visual signals to supplicate or to challenge others of the same species, although sometimes the behaviour appears to be incongruous. During a dispute, birds will often break off hostilities and begin to feed, or at least pretend to feed. This is known as 'displacement activity', and it refers to normal behaviour at an inappropriate time.

Birds also begin activities but do not complete them, a form of behaviour that is known as 'intention movement'. Before taking off, a bird usually stretches its neck, but one that is a little nervous, perhaps having spotted a distant predator, will stretch its neck and not take off. It signals its intention to fly, but, reassured by subsequent events, such as the predator flying past without attacking, finds it unnecessary to complete the task. Taking this a stage further, birds will also stretch their necks simply because they feel uncomfortable, whether there is danger present or not.

THE POWER OF RITUAL

Many of the movements and postures in a bird's repertoire of signals resemble movements they make as part of their everyday behaviour, such as preening, feeding or drinking. During courtship, some species of duck throw the head back in a way that resembles preening movements when oiling feathers. In the display the preening

function has been lost; the behaviour has become a 'ritual' which reassures the other bird that it has friendly intentions. If a bird is doing something that is very ordinary it is unlikely to attack.

In some species of bird, the ritualised

BENEFITS OF A LONG TAIL

Tails feature strongly in the displays of Africa's long-tailed widow birds. The male has red flashes on his wings and a bunch of tail feathers about twice the length of his body. The display involves the male flying low over the savannah grassland and showing off his tail to the assembled females. In an experiment some males had their tails artificially lengthened by gluing on extra pieces. These extra-long tails clearly conferred an advantage on the recipients, who enticed twice as many females into their territories as their rivals.

display is enhanced by special markings or structures. Male ducks integrate preening into their displays and often the movement directs a female's attention to an area of eye-catching plumage. The mallard lifts a wing and reveals brightly coloured feathers.

Other birds have all kinds of advertisements. Blue-footed boobies have, as their name suggests, big blue feet that they wave at their partner. Sulphur-crested cockatoos raise a sulphur-coloured crest of feathers on top of their head. And the most elaborate illustrations of natural selection gone wild – the peacock and the argus pheasant – raise enormous fan-like tails into the air and rattle their quills.

Imitating young birds is another way to appease a potential mate. A pair of gulls walk alongside each other tossing their heads and making a quiet call. This behaviour resembles the begging behaviour of a juvenile gull and triggers the concerned response of a diligent parent rather than the aggressive approach of a potential rival.

Several of these types of behaviour may be combined in a complex display to attract and appease a partner: the great crested grebe, for example, engages in one of the most elaborate of courtship displays. The first stage may be a simple head-shaking display with erect crests – a form of behaviour that has evolved from the head-turning movement when one bird turns away from another as it changes from aggression to appeasement. A second stage might see one bird diving while the other

GREBE DISPLAY *Great crested grebes appear to walk on water and shake heads during their 'weed dance'.*

sits at the surface with its wings open and its crests erect. This may progress as the diving bird surfaces and stands almost erect in front of the other bird. What often follows is the 'weed dance' in which the two birds dive below to collect weed from the bottom of the lake and swim towards each other. They then rise vertically from the surface of the water with the weed in their beaks, keeping themselves erect by paddling rapidly with their feet and shaking their heads violently. The weed display is a throwback to the movements involved in nest building.

Ritualised displays are not, of course, confined to birds. Humans gesticulate when speaking to emphasise the meaning or status of a word. Often we yawn not because we are tired but to show we are bored. And we blush not because increased blood flow to the face is going to help us out of difficulty, but because our body signals involuntarily that we are embarrassed. All these forms of ritualised behaviour are means of nonverbal communication similar to the displays of other animals.

BOOBY DANCING *The male blue-footed booby points to the sky, opens his wings and raises his big blue feet in a courtship display.*

LIP SMACKING OR BARED TEETH: THE SECRETS OF THE FACE

More than 100 years ago, Charles Darwin published *The Expression of the Emotions in Man and Animals*. In it, he pointed out that many creatures, including dogs, cats, monkeys, apes and humans, have facial expressions. He believed that our repertoire of facial expressions had evolved from those of our non-human ancestors – the monkeys and apes.

A body language involving the face is only possible in mammals, because this group alone has the lips, cheeks, pliable skin and facial muscles to allow a rich repertoire of facial expressions to develop. And of the mammals only a few groups have perfected the necessary movements of the lips, corners of the mouth, eyes, eyelids, eyebrows, skin of the forehead and ears. The movements, which may well have evolved from everyday needs, have become ritualised, although it is often hard to see what their original function might have been. Laughing, crying and smiling are examples of facial expressions that have so far resisted such examination.

The way in which facial elements are used varies from species to species. People and macaques raise their eyebrows, whereas apes rarely do. A human has a deeper frown than a chimpanzee but the chimp

In a Quandary With a forefinger pressed to its cheek, a lowland gorilla is the picture of puzzlement.

has a broader grin – and chimp 'grins' are expressions of fear rather than pleasure. Some species have developed skin colours that accentuate movement, such as light-coloured eyelids that seem to glow when an animal flashes them. Nevertheless, the range of facial displays is limited in all species.

There are about eight distinct facial displays. The 'tense-mouth face' shows aggression and must be seen as a threat. The 'staring open-mouth face' is a warning that the animal will bite if approached. 'Bared-teeth faces', varying from a 'staring bared-teeth scream face' to a 'high-intensity' one with a frown, both accompanied by a scream, happen when an animal has had something withheld by a stronger animal – a sign of frustration. A 'silent bared-teeth face' is shown by a dominant animal to subordinates, informing the latter that it is not hostile (much like a human smile). The 'lip-smacking face' expresses friendliness; the 'pout face' shows helplessness; and the 'relaxed open-mouth face' is used during play.

Humans do not use the lip-

smacking display, but have two additional facial expressions associated with contempt and surprise. Otherwise, we share with the rest of the monkeys and apes the full range of primate facial expressions: smiling, for example, is a specimen of a silent bared-teeth display and laughing is a relaxed open-mouth display.

At Rest A young chimpanzee has a relaxed face.

Excited A chimp with a low, closed grin shows excitement.

Power The face of a dominant male silverback gorilla.

Threat Display A lowland gorilla shows his canine teeth.

TOUCH, ELECTRICITY AND SMELL

Touch conveys intimate messages. Animals that have trouble finding one another in the first place use electricity to communicate. For announcements that need to last, leaving a scent-trace is effective.

Just after the Sun goes down in parts of Africa and Asia, the ghostly yells and yaps of a pair of jackals will pierce the darkness. They are proclaiming the patch of territory they will defend aggressively against any intruders. The exception is when they are following a pride of hunting lions, in which case they remain silent until the lions have made their kill. Then the jackals erupt in a wailing chorus. They are very noisy animals who bicker continuously among themselves.

JACKAL GREETINGS *Black-backed jackals use body language, smell and touch to exchange greetings.*

When they meet for the first time, however, they use a more intimate form of communication: touch. One jackal approaches the other not head-on, which would indicate an aggressive attitude, but from an angle. The second jackal greets the first by raising a paw and touching it on the shoulder. It is a gesture that 'tests' the other's friendliness. The first animal responds by pivoting its body around to rub its rump against the other's and then hits it several times on the shoulder, much like a person patting another on the back. This greeting ceremony is one of the ways in which jackals avoid serious physical confrontation. The first animal, a dominant one, establishes his status over the second, or subordinate jackal, using touch, not sound or vision.

TOUCH TESTING

Like many of the higher animals, jackals use most available channels of communication. They have loud howls, barks and yaps that can be heard over long distances. They use scent marks that act as semi-permanent calling cards or territorial 'keep out' signs. And they have visual signals such as facial expressions, hair bristling and tail wagging. When an intimate liaison is needed, the ultimate test is by touch. The sides of the mouth and the groin area are particularly sensitive and touching in these areas is associated with friendliness.

Touch is a signalling system that must be used at very close quarters. Most often, it is seen during the very last stages of courtship, after other communication systems have brought a pair of animals together. A male frog or toad calls for his mate, but when contact has been made he makes a grab for

FOR THE LOVE OF A TOAD *In Costa Rica, toads (opposite) jostle for the right to mate with a female.*

FLIPPER PAT *A male Galápagos sea lion reassures one of his harem by resting his flipper on her body.*

his new partner and, in a form of behaviour known as 'amplexus', hangs on for all he is worth. Touch then encourages the female to spawn.

Among the higher animals, touch not only stimulates a partner but also conveys reassurance. A female tayra – a South American relative of the marten – will groom a male, licking his ears and scratching his head with her forepaws. Touch may, however, have the opposite effect as with the unreceptive female polecat who

PEACE AND GROOMING *Grey langurs in northern India groom each other and encourage social harmony.*

rebuffs an ardent suitor with little chin bites and neck nips.

Under the sea, touch is important to whales and dolphins. In close encounters they touch with their flippers, rub their bodies together and press genital organs against a neighbour, even though it may not be of the opposite sex or even an animal of the same species. The tactile sense is also important for the dugong and manatee – marine mammals living in coastal tropical waters. They have sensitive whiskers on the muzzle that are used not only during feeding but also during courtship. In one encounter in a river on the Florida coast, a manatee was seen to nuzzle its partner's side and then put its flipper on the other's back. This use of the flipper in maintaining body contact is also seen in seals and sea lions. Whisker-to-whisker contact, though, is an aggressive signal in fur seals.

WELL GROOMED

Tactile communication appears to have reached its zenith in the primates. It starts immediately after birth. The positive feedback received by a baby from its mother enables the young to grow up normally and is a form of communication that the

DOLPHIN NUZZLE *Spotted dolphins (opposite) touch, nuzzle and play with one another constantly.*

animal will use throughout its life. The way is by no means clear-cut, however, for the youngster will learn that touch signals can both attract and repel, and the same signal can deliver both messages depending on the context or the individual. An adult stump-tailed macaque will push with its hand to create space between two individuals, but a juvenile macaque uses the same signal to invite play.

Contact can be simple. Marmosets, tamarins and night monkeys, for example, huddle together in holes in trees, which not only keeps them warm but also helps to develop and maintain group cohesion. Bonds between individuals may be reinforced when the animals intertwine their tails. Hugging or embracing serves as a greeting that reduces aggression. Mothers carry their babies, of course, but juveniles and males will also carry one another. At the same time they will also nuzzle and groom each other.

Grooming is probably the most

PLEASING THE BOSS *Subordinate olive baboons often groom more dominant ones.*

ROMEO CALLING *The smaller male* Argiope *spider from southern Europe plucks gently but regularly on the female's web.*

East African baboons, for example, will groom each other after a fight. Similarly, a West African female talapoin monkey of high rank will intercede during a confrontation between the dominant male and a subordinate, grooming the high-ranking male to calm him down. And a talapoin mother who is being harassed by an infant will distract its attention by grooming it. Male talapoins have an unusual way of saying 'thank you'. They pay back the individual grooming them by hitting its coat in a symbolic but rather brutal form of grooming.

GOOD VIBRATIONS

Web spiders have a form of communication that might be described as 'touch at a distance'. The everyday use of a web is as a trap for prey, but for the male spider it is also his means of approaching a female without being eaten. The male garden spider – one of the orb weavers – signals his intention to the female by plucking certain strings on her web. Some species produce and pluck their own thread, which they attach to the female's web.

The vibrations are delivered in a set pattern, unlike the irregular struggling movements of prey. The tune a male plays is important for his survival, for if he puts a foot wrong and she receives inappropriate vibrations he will end up dead. She must respond to the male by shaking her web with a distinctive signal. The female, however, may be in for a shock. One species – the cannibalistic spider-eating spider, *Ero furcata* – has learned how to imitate the vibrations of certain male web spiders and uses this to approach, capture and eat their females.

Male pondskaters or water striders use vibrations, in the form of ripples on the surface of freshwater ponds, to repel rivals and advertise their availability to females during courtship. This takes place at leks (special breeding grounds). Males and females gather at the aquatic display arena, with the males taking up positions on suitable signalling sites, such as a small twig. Each male produces ripples by waving one of its pairs of legs up and down on the

important kind of tactile signal exchanged by monkeys, and it varies from species to species. Mother baboons, langurs and macaques groom their infants, whereas guenons – long-tailed African monkeys –

tend to start when their youngsters are older. Most adult females groom more often and for longer than adult males, although male baboons and macaques are active in social grooming. It appears to be a very pleasurable experience and it clearly goes beyond the everyday function of cleaning. It establishes, maintains and reinforces contact between individuals and reduces tension in a closely knit group.

PHEROMONES: A MOST SUBTLE PERFUME

Female silk moths produce pheromones. These are chemical messengers that an animal releases into the environment to influence the behaviour and physiology of another individual of the same species. Translated from the Greek, pheromones are substances that 'transfer excitement', and in moths minute quantities of these airborne chemicals transfer excitement from females to males. The amounts are so small that in order to obtain about 1/2500 oz (12 mg) for analysis in the laboratory, scientists have had to extract the scent glands of more than half a million moths.

How the communication system works has now been established. The female moth raises her abdomen, protrudes a pair of glands, releases the pheromone and flutters her wings to waft it into the air. The wind does the rest. A plume of scent spreads downwind and by the time it reaches a male of the same species it may be considerably diluted. The male, however, who may be over 2 miles (3 km) away, can detect just a single molecule, if it lands on his feathery antennae.

On the male moth's antennae there are 60 000 minute hairs, and more than three-quarters of them are tuned in to respond to the female's scent – a compound with the tongue-twisting name of 'trans-10-cis-12-hexacadien-1-ol', otherwise known as bombykol. Receptor cells are constantly being fired on the antennae. So, although the cells are capable of registering just one molecule of bombykol, it requires about 200 molecules to land on the antennae before the male moth's brain recognises that there is a female broadcasting her availability upwind of him. Aroused by sufficient pheromones, the male moth changes direction and flies upwind in a series of zigzags to the source of the odour.

How, though, does he home in on

TRACKING DOWN *The male emperor moth tracks down a female by following her scent.*

his intended? There are many females in the vicinity and they are all producing pheromones. The crosstalk could be very confusing. The solution is to encode the delivery of the pheromones: the perfume is released in short bursts. The female North American bella moth, for example, puffs out her aphrodisiac at a rate of 1 1/2 puffs per second. The pulsed effect ensures that the male moth has sufficient information to locate and mate with the moth of his dreams.

FEELERS FOR PHEROMONES *The male emperor gum moth uses its feathery antennae to detect minute quantities of the female's scent.*

water's surface. He will also defend his site against rivals, for it is here that the females will lay their eggs. Males send aggressive signals rippling across the surface at 85-90 waves per second, but the courtship signal is much slower. Twenty-two ripples per second will win over a female, and her ripple discrimination is so acute that she can distinguish signals just 1 1/2 ripples apart at a distance of 16-24 in (40-60 cm) from the signaller.

Blind mole rats, meanwhile, communicate by producing shocks and vibrations similar to mini-earthquakes. They live alone in burrows under the savannah of east Africa and do not tolerate others of their kind. Confrontation could mean a fight to

the death and so each animal, which has no visible eyes, ears or tail, keeps in touch with its rivals with vibrations through the soil. It makes them in a most peculiar way, by banging its head on the roof of its burrow. It strikes the soil four times within a half-second and repeats the sequence several times in succession. It then rests its jaw on the side of the tunnel in order to pick up the vibrations of any mole rat that

ROYAL SCENT *The entire life of the naked mole rat is dominated by a scent given off by the 'queen' mole rat.*

happens to answer. In this way each mole rat establishes the position of its neighbour and avoids the possibility of meeting it.

If we could detect the electrical and magnetic events that take place in the

natural world, we would 'see' an entirely different world. It is a world that is denied to us, but is explored and exploited by creatures that live under water.

SHOCK TACTICS

Fish are the major inhabitants of the electric environment. There are fish, such as sharks and rays, that detect minute quantities of electrical activity in the bodies of their prey, even though they may be buried in the sand. There are those, such as the electric ray, the electric catfish and the electric eel, that produce their own current from modified muscles and are able to stun their prey with a strong electrical discharge. And there are those, such as blue sharks, that can navigate across the ocean with reference to the Earth's geo-magnetic field. But the most interesting of the electric fish are those that 'talk' using electricity.

Some electric fishes, such as Africa's elephant trunkfish, find their way about in turbid waters using their electricity. They surround themselves with a weak electric field and anything that enters the field causes interference, which gives the fish information

ELECTRIC DETECTORS A blue shark (left) can detect minute electrical fields produced by its prey. The long-nosed elephant trunkfish (below) uses a weak electric field for navigation and communication.

PULSE AND WAVE The elephant fish (top) discharges electricity in bursts or pulses, the knife fish (above) in high-frequency waves.

about the position of the obstacle. Each species has its own rate of discharge, with some as high as 1800 pulses per second. It also uses the electrical activity as a signal to other electric fish, and electrocommunication has been found to parallel other modes of communication to the extent that scientists now talk about 'electrolanguages'.

Fundamental to communication is the ability to transmit information about the identity of the individual. This includes its species, gender, stage of development and age, and useful motivational data such as readiness to mate, proclamation of territory, spacing signals and an indication of how strong the prospective mate is. Weak electric fish have distinctive patterns of discharges for many of these functions.

There are two types of signallers, the 'pulse species', which communicate with bursts of electrical activity at low-discharge rates, and 'wave species', which speak with more continuous, high-frequency discharges. Many of the pulsed species deliver their signals in distinctive patterns that are repeated for long periods, sometimes for 10-20 minutes.

The elephant trunkfish, for example, has a characteristic code with discharges that rise after 25 milliseconds, drop, then rise again steeply at 100 milliseconds, and tail off at 250 milliseconds. The African knife fish, on the other hand, is a wave species and broadcasts at 50-150 Hz. Males and females are on different frequencies –

males at 50-90 Hz and females at 100-150 Hz. Youngsters in the nest communicate with their parents on guard outside on the 80 Hz waveband. During sexual or aggressive encounters, the discharge rate rises significantly, and a very angry knife fish can be provoked into silence followed by a very hostile 'attack pattern'. There are even electrocommunication manners: if two fish broadcasting on the same frequency meet they avoid jamming each other's signal by shifting the frequency slightly.

WHAT'S IN A SMELL?

Sounds and sights, touches and shocks are fleeting forms of communication. If a message is to last, a creature must resort to producing odours and to scent-marking. A wide range of animals use the technique: it is a way in which an animal can pass a signal to another of the same species without having to stay around to deliver it. It is often used to mark territorial boundaries or demarcate living areas. Honeybees scent

RHINO TRACES *The black rhino tramples dung and spreads the scent on the soles of its feet.*

the entrance to their hive and also leave odour trails around rich sources of food. Bumblebees have regular circuits that are marked by odours, and weaver ants leave faecal spots to identify territorial preserves.

But the best-studied scent markers are mammals. The European rabbit deposits 800 droppings a day to mark its territory. The hippopotamus, with its whirling, muck-spreading tail, liberally distributes its dung in rivers running through its territory and around the territory's land boundaries. The black rhinoceros places piles of dung at strategic points along its trails. The scent is spread about even more when the rhino tramples the dung and takes the smell along on the soles of its feet. Some lorises, lemurs and New World monkeys urinate on their feet, spreading their odour signal over the trees through which they travel. The acrobatic dwarf mongoose stands on its head to daub a secretion from the anal gland onto the highest parts of bushes and rocks – the

higher the spot, the bigger the creature appears to be. Hamsters and gerbils rub their flanks and undersides on rocks and logs, and burrowing rodents rub their flanks against the walls of their tunnels.

Among the more unusual scent markers are the dwarf antelopes of Africa, such as the oribi and the dik-dik. They live in stable groups consisting of a male accompanied by several females. They maintain an exclusive territory and have scent glands with which to put out their boundary markers. There are several glands on various parts of the body. Sticky secretions from glands in front of the eyes are smeared on to grass stems. Glands under the hoofs mark the ground along well-used pathways. The oribi, which has six gland sites, even has a scent gland close to its ear.

The domestic dog is an avid scent marker. Its wild counterpart, the wolf, does the same. The territory of a pack of timber wolves is marked by a boundary line of urine 'keep out' signs. The sense of smell is not only important for sending messages to other packs, it is also one means by which animals in the same pack disseminate information. Urination passes messages between pack members as a kind of group bond. In the mating season, for instance, the dominant female will issue chemical bulletins in her urine about her readiness to mate. As one leading wolf researcher once remarked: 'Wolves that pee together, stay together.'

The smelling abilities of the dog family – wolves, foxes, dholes, dingoes and African wild dogs – are well known. The secret lies in their nasal passages. In

ON PATROL IN LEMUR TERRITORY *Groups of ring-tailed lemurs living in wooded areas of Madagascar use smell to mark out their territories. A female lemur (right) sniffs a marking post for signs of a rival gang.*

humans, two sheets of yellow-coloured, mucus-moistened olfactory epithelium – smell membrane – in the two nasal passages contain about 5 million sensory receptor cells, whereas the dog has intricately folded sheets that would cover an area 50 times as great if unfolded and which contain more than 220 million

MAMMALS LIKE INSECTS

Naked mole rats are unusual mammals since they behave like social insects. They live in large underground colonies and have an all-powerful queen. She produces a scent or pheromone, much like that of a queen honeybee, which ensures that she suppresses reproduction in other females and is therefore the only breeding female. The rest of the mole rats are 'workers', engaged in tunnel construction, food gathering, defence and so on. The nonbreeding members are not sterile, allowing a dominant worker to replace the queen if she dies.

sensory cells. The dog's nose is also built for intensive smelling, the long nasal passages allowing air to circulate around the smell membranes.

The odours produced by dogs give in-

formation to other dogs about their sex, pack and age; they also mark out partners and territories. The lives of other hunters are dominated by smell, too. The African spotted hyena, for example, has a special scent-producing anal gland. When two hyenas meet they protrude their anal glands in greeting and lift a hind leg so that each may sniff and lick the other's genital area. The gland also produces a pungent paste, known to local people as witches' butter. It is deposited on grass stems at the height of a hyena's nose and serves as a territorial marker, telling other hyena clans to keep out.

While the smell sense of a human is clearly inferior to that of a dog, human noses can still be remarkably sensitive. A skilled perfumier, for instance, can distinguish up to 10 000

WALLOWING HIPPOS
Hippopotamuses use dung to mark out their territories.

TWIG SNIFFER *An African klipspringer antelope sniffs for scent markers left by other klipspringers.*

distinct odours. There is some evidence, too, that pheromones play a part in human society. The members of a tribe in New Guinea, for example, do not shake hands when parting company. Instead, the friends rub their hands under the armpit and exchange smells.

ANIMALS AND PEOPLE

5

SAY 'PAPA' *In experiments in 1909, an orang-utan was trained to say 'papa' and 'cup'.*

ANIMALS HAVE LONG FASCINATED AND ENTERTAINED HUMAN BEINGS, WHETHER IN CIRCUSES OR ZOOS, ON THE STAGE OR THE SCREEN, IN THE DOMESTIC ENVIRONMENT OR THE CREATURES' NATURAL HABITATS. SOME ARE INVITED TO SHARE PEOPLE'S LIVES AS PETS, WHILE OTHERS ARE TRAINED TO HELP, AS POLICE DOGS, SAY, OR GUIDE DOGS FOR THE BLIND. AN UNFORTUNATE FEW ARE EXPLOITED, WHEREAS OTHERS ARE CHERISHED, OFTEN MOLLYCODDLED. BUT WHEREVER AND WHENEVER PEOPLE MAKE CONTACT WITH ANIMALS, IN THE HOME OR IN THE WILD, THERE HAS ALWAYS BEEN A CURIOUS AND ALMOST IRRESISTIBLE DESIRE ON THE PART OF THE HUMANS TO TAP INTO THE ANIMALS' MINDS AND EVEN TO TRY TO TALK TO THEM.

MAN AND HORSE *A ploughing match in Surrey, England.*

TRAINED TO SERVE

Human beings have harnessed the natural skills and habits of many animals. Animals have been used to direct trains, detect contraband, fly space rockets, carry goods and go fishing and hunting.

A man's best friend, so the saying goes, is his dog . . . or maybe his pig, monkey, horse, camel, buffalo, eagle or cormorant. Animals have been honed to perfection over millions of years of evolution to live and thrive in the niche that nature has reserved for them. Their senses, skills and patterns of behaviour have all evolved to fulfil a particular role.

Some, like rats and cockroaches, have developed bodies and ways of behaving that enable them to live just about anywhere, to adapt to any circumstance and to exploit any opportunity. Often they are in competition with humankind, which is composed, after all, of just another group of generalists and opportunists. Some, such as monkeys and apes, are so similar in make-up to humankind that they can be dragooned into switching places with us. Other animals, such as dogs, dolphins and birds of prey, are highly specialised.

Some of their senses are fine-tuned to enable them to exploit opportunities that are denied to others, including humans, and so man, the eternal entrepreneur, has sought to collaborate rather than compete with these species. And just as animals understand lessons taught to them by parents and elders, they also seem capable of appreciating the

TRAINED FOR COCONUTS *Pig-tailed macaques in Thailand are taught to climb trees and recover coconuts.*

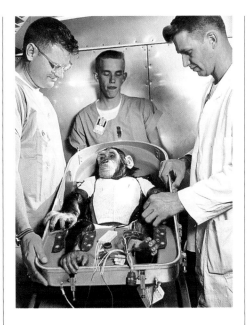

CHIMPS IN SPACE *Ham the chimp during training for a space flight (left). Monkeys were often used in early space flights (above).*

lessons taught them by humans. The liaison has sometimes been quite bizarre.

In 1959, Able and Baker – respectively, a rhesus macaque and a squirrel monkey – became the first animals to survive outside the planet when the US space agency NASA shot them, at speeds of up to 10 000 mph (16 000 km/h), 300 miles (480 km) into space where they experienced 38 times the pull of gravity. Many other animals had preceded them into space but Able and Baker were the first to come back alive. The 'monkeynauts' were stand-ins for human astronauts. If monkeys could survive the forces of takeoff and re-entry and live in a state of weightlessness without damage, then perhaps humans could too. They were surrogate humans, and were required to do very little.

SPACE TRAVEL

Ham, on the other hand, was an operator. Ham, until January 31, 1961, was known simply as Test Subject Number 61. He was an experimental chimpanzee required by NASA to work a variety of switches in response to flashing lights while flying in his Mercury capsule, orbiting at a speed of 5800 mph (9300 km/h) about 155 miles

SIGNAL BABOON *In the 1880s Jack the baboon changed the railway signals for his disabled companion.*

(250 km) up in space. If he did not complete a task he would receive a mild electric shock. Ham did so well that despite experiencing a force that was equal to 17 times his body weight on takeoff, running short of oxygen during the flight and nearly drowning at splashdown, he experienced only three shocks during the entire

flight. Ham the Space Chimp became an unwitting celebrity.

It is not surprising that monkeys and apes should deputise for humans. They are our nearest relatives, and the chimpanzee shares with us about 99 per cent of its genetic make-up. In pharmaceutical and cosmetics laboratories, in car-crash tests and in military research this closeness in physical make-up and behaviour has proved something of a handicap for seemingly intelligent nonhuman primates. But in the late 19th century it enabled one particular primate to use his 'intelligence' for the good of his human companion.

Jack was a chacma baboon who belonged to James Wide, a railway worker in South Africa. Wide had lost his legs in a railway accident but was kept on by the company as a signalman at Uitenhage in the Cape. Although he could get around on wooden legs, he still needed help, so he trained the baboon to do his job. The animal could pull signal levers and fetch the relevant keys in response to whistle signals from an approaching train. He could also pump water from a well, do some

HELPING HUMANS *Monkeys have been trained to carry out chores for handicapped people.*

gardening and push Wide to and from work on a specially designed railway trolley that the baboon put on and took off the rails twice a day. The baboon was considered to be very 'intelligent'. He learned the signal levers as well as his master. Although passengers were, not surprisingly,

TO THE RESCUE *Dogs sniff out and locate people buried in rubble after a Sicilian earthquake.*

a little apprehensive about a baboon operating the signals, Jack never got it wrong. He became so competent that the company took him onto the payroll. He earned a small sum of money each week and received a half-bottle of beer on Saturdays.

Similarly, in the 1970s Johnnie, a pet rhesus macaque, learned how to drive a tractor on a farm at Balmoral in Australia. He would respond correctly to driving instructions such as 'turn left' and 'turn right'. The farmer stood in a trailer behind the tractor dishing out fodder to livestock while the monkey drove them along.

MONKEY PAGE-TURNER

On some tropical islands monkeys are trained to climb trees and harvest coconuts. And primates, particularly monkeys, have been trained to assist people with disabilities. A quadriplegic victim of a car crash in Rhode Island, USA, for example, lives a more normal life with the help of a South American capuchin monkey. The monkey was raised from birth with a human family, where it learned to assist its human companion to turn the pages of a book, search for objects and help him to eat meals.

Using animals to help people with disabilities is not unusual. The patience and placidity of a labrador dog make it an ideal companion-guide for a blind person. The dog undergoes an extensive training programme that enables it to be dependable when dealing with complicated situations, such as crossing a busy road. But without its natural intelligence, the dog would not understand its master's commands. Dogs show an ability to learn. They can be taught to recognise signals and to associate a signal with a particular task or piece of behaviour.

The dog is in reality a domesticated wolf and its wild ancestry is much in evidence in the home or on the street or farm. The wolf's hunting tactic of separating a victim from a herd, for example, is exploited by shepherds in training sheepdogs. Its innate aggression and ferocity have been put to use by the police for crowd control and by the military and security firms in the form of guard dogs. The dog has inherited the wolf's remarkable sense of smell, its ability to detect the faintest odours. This has been put to good use in tracking criminals, finding people buried in avalanches or victims trapped under rubble after an earthquake, and in sniffing out explosives and narcotics.

The dog has been bred to play these

TRUFFLE SNUFFLERS *Pigs are used in the south of France to sniff out valuable truffles.*

TRAINED TO FISH *Cormorants are specially bred in China to catch and regurgitate fish for their owners.*

roles for thousands of years – its domesticated origins date to between 10 000 and 35 000 years ago. The pig, by contrast, was bred to be eaten. But pigs have, it seems, a sense of smell that is as acute as a dog's, an ability that has been put to good use in parts of France during the yearly truffle season. The pig's natural tendency to

snuffle about on the forest floor and dig out underground roots, tubers and fungi is ideal for unearthing valuable black, warty-looking truffles.

While pigs are probably the least easy farm animals to train, horses are probably the most receptive. Like dogs, they have a great capacity to learn signals and commands and have been used as transport and to pull carts and ploughs. Similarly, elephants in southern Asia can be trained to perform a variety of useful tasks, from taking part in religious ceremonies and processions to hauling tree trunks through the forest. An

Asian elephant trained for logging has to perform up to 40 different types of manoeuvre in the course of a day's work.

Perhaps the most unusual way in which humans have exploited an animal's natural skills and abilities is demonstrated by Japanese and Chinese fishermen. In a fishing technique that has changed very little for hundreds of years, they harness the underwater hunting skills of the cormorant. The bird is trained to swim down to a shoal of fish, grab one and swim back to the fishing boat. A leather collar around its neck prevents it from swallowing the catch. The fisherman gently squeezes the bird's upper throat and the fish is regurgitated. The cormorant is then encouraged to dive

LOG BEARERS *Elephants have traditionally been used in southern Asia in the logging industry.*

FALCONRY — A SPORT FOR COMMONERS

The origins of falconry go back more than 4000 years in central Asia. It was not at first the sport of the nobility, but a means for ordinary people to secure meat in a harsh landscape where early stock farming was unreliable.

The bond between falconer and bird was – and is – based simply on food. Like their human neighbours, falcons living in the semidesert regions of central Asia had a hard time. People carried them to the locations where they stood the best chance of securing a meal and by sharing the spoils guaranteed them a daily food supply.

Unlike dogs, which hunt out of eagerness to please the 'pack leader', falcons hunt only when they are hungry. So falconers learned to recognise a falcon's weight and moods. They found that a bird must be fed sufficient meat to ensure its health and survival, but not enough to blunt its eagerness to hunt. Lean and keen birds will hunt and kill bustards, grouse and hares, while well-fed birds will not.

Birds are trained to accept their handler and to fly to a falconer in return for a reward of food. Then they are allowed to fly free to perfect their strength and flying abilities. After that, they are recalled once more for their food. Eventually, the birds are taken out to hunt for themselves. After a catch, it is notoriously difficult to separate a falcon from its hard-won meal. The falconer must lure it away with alternative morsels.

Traditionally, the birds of central Asia were caught and trained in the autumn, and used to hunt during the winter when meat was scarce. Many free birds would have had to face the hazards of long-distance migration, but a falconer's charge was assured a daily food supply close to its spring and summer breeding grounds. With the arrival of

spring, life became easier and the falcons were released to fend for themselves and to breed naturally.

MAN AND BIRD *Wings outstretched, a falcon perches on its trainer's gloved hand.*

---

in to catch more. Its motivation to do so is that the fisherman allows it to eat every eighth fish. If the fisherman forgets to give the bird the eighth fish, it refuses to dive.

WILD COMPANIONS

A remarkable partnership between wild, untamed animals and humans developed at Twofold Bay on the coast of New South Wales, Australia. Each winter a pod (or school) of killer whales, including a large male that the locals nicknamed Old Tom, arrived in the bay. They were joined by whalers from the small town of Eden, and whales and people hunted together. Their quarry consisted of humpback and fin whales that migrated into the area every year. A giant whale was driven close to the shore, where the killer whales harassed it, grabbing its tail and smothering its blow-hole until it was tired and breathless. Then

the whalers would kill it using their long-handled lances and harpoons. The victim dropped to the sea floor, where the killer whales vied for the best bit – the tongue and lips. The whale fishermen waited until gases filled the dead animal's insides and it rose to the surface. They then towed it to the shore and sliced it up.

One thing was particularly curious about the behaviour of Old Tom's pod. If humpback whales appeared, several members of the pod surrounded the target while a couple of others went to raise the alarm. They swam to Eden and slapped their flippers and flukes on the water surface to attract the attention of the whalers and then led them out to sea to the place where the others had trapped their quarry.

Cooperation between wild cetaceans (whales and dolphins) and people is well documented. In Roman times, Pliny the

Elder, who died during the eruption of Vesuvius in AD 79, tells of dolphins that helped fishermen by driving shoals of fish into their nets. Modern-day experts were sceptical of Pliny's observations until they discovered just such a thing happening on the coast of Mauritania in north-west Africa. There, the Imgrarguen people have been cooperating with dolphins for their daily catch for hundreds of years.

The villagers wait for the arrival of fish and dolphins in September, when the mullet are heading south. As the first shoals appear in the shallows, the local children splash the water with sticks to summon the dolphins. The first sign is a row of dorsal fins on the sea's surface. The hunting school might be 100 strong and they swim about 65-100 ft (20-30 m) out, parallel to the shore, driving the mullet ahead of them. The fishermen race into the water carrying their hand-woven nets, some wading up to their chests. They block the escape route of the fish, which jump out of the water, surrounding the men with flashes of silver. The dolphins weave in and out of the men's legs, avoiding the nets and taking their share of the catch.

At Laguna in southern Brazil, 30 to 40 fishermen go fishing with dolphins nearly every day of the year, selling their catch commercially at local markets. The fishing pattern follows a tradition that was first recorded in 1847. The fishermen, each carrying a circular net, wade out and stand in a line parallel to the shore. The water is murky and so they rely on the dolphins to know where to throw their nets. The dolphins first appear some distance away but slowly swim towards the men. One by one, they submerge and swim closer. Suddenly a dolphin will emerge from the water just in front of a fisherman and turn on its side. This is the signal for the man to cast his net. If the dolphin does not turn, the fisherman will not cast. The dolphins, it seems, lead the hunt, dictating by their position where the men should stand and when they should begin to fish. Their reward, if the fishing is good, is 20-25 lb (10-12 kg) of mullet a day, which they catch easily in the confusion amongst the nets.

DOLPHIN RESCUE

As well as ancient stories about dolphins and fishermen working together, there are many myths and legends about dolphins rescuing people. Around 700 BC the Greek poet Arion was supposed to have been rescued by dolphins when he jumped into the sea to escape pirates. These stories were given some degree of respectability after an event that took place off the isolated Halftide Beach in New South Wales, Australia, in January 1989.

Three boys were surfing amongst a school of dolphins. Suddenly, the dolphins became agitated and started to mill around the surfboards. Then, in an eruption of foam, a shark – possibly a great white shark, the largest predatory fish in the sea – lunged out of the water, taking a chunk out of a board and out of a boy. Blood streamed into the water and the boy lashed out to try to discourage the shark. At this moment the dolphins began to splash the water and ram the shark with their snouts, driving it away while the boys limped back with their injured fellow to the shore. The boys were saved from almost certain death.

But were the dolphins engaged in some altruistic act or were they merely defending themselves, with the boys benefiting by chance? Another incident at Delagoa Bay in Mozambique suggests that dolphins may indeed deliberately help people in distress.

The victim was a 20-year-old girl from Pretoria who had cut her foot in a boating accident. Blood in the water attracted several sharks. Without warning, two dolphins appeared. They not only chased away the sharks but supported the girl as she struggled to reach a shipping buoy. She was totally exhausted and at first was unable to climb onto the buoy. The dolphins remained alongside her until she was able to haul herself from the water. A lookout on a passing oil tanker spotted her, radioed for help and a rescue boat took her ashore.

TEAMWORK *Dolphins cooperate with human fishermen to herd and catch fish at Laguna on the Brazilian coast. It is not known how the collaboration arose.*

CREATURES THAT PERFORM

Since humans first tamed them, animals have had a place at home and while hunting. They have also been entertainers – and the more they perform like humans, the more intelligent they are deemed to be.

From earliest times, people have been entertained by animals, whether in 'sports' such as fox-hunting, stag-hunting and hare-coursing, or other diversions, such as watching performing animals in circuses, dolphinaria, zoos and fairs, or following the form in horse-racing, or being enthralled by the combined talents of man and beast in sheepdog trials and horse shows. Whatever the amusement, hunters and audiences alike are struck by the way in which animals are clever enough to avoid being caught, or can be taught to perform remarkable tricks and stunts, or encouraged to achieve extraordinary feats of speed and skill.

The thrill of the hunt and the spectacle of an animal show are combined in bullfighting, which the American writer Ernest Hemingway described as 'the only art in which the artist is in danger of death'. Bullfighting is thought to have originated several thousand years ago in the Spanish province of Andalusia. In 228 BC, when Carthaginians and Romans were carving up the Mediterranean world between them, stories came out of Iberia of men who used skins or cloaks to avoid being gored to death by savage bulls that

SIAMESE BULLS *Fighting bulls provide the entertainment in an arena in Thailand.*

they then killed single-handed with axes or lances.

Today the bulls are not wild but bred on special farms or *ganaderías*, though they are thought to be the descendants of an aggressive race of wild cattle that lived in the forests of the Iberian Peninsula. They are selected not only for their ferocity and fighting ability, but also for their intelligence. It is one thing to be fit and strong but quite another to be able to focus that energy in a way that will provide the best 'sport' for the spectators. Young bulls are tested for their alertness and fighting ability during their first year. Only those showing the necessary spirit are saved for the *corrida de toros* or reserved for breeding.

Cattle are colour-blind, seeing shades of grey rather than distinct colours. But it is also perfectly true that a bull reacts to having something red waved at it. In tests, bulls have shown that they can distinguish between feeding troughs marked by different-coloured flags. They do not see 'red', rather a particular shade of grey. Fighting bulls, bursting with aggressive genes and trained to charge at people waving large red rags, are in no doubt about what to do when they see a matador with a red-lined cape. They are also taunted by the movements of the cape and the gestures and postures of the bullfighter.

In Spain, despite all the breeding, bulls fight only once. After the 'hour of truth' (the bullfight), they are hauled unceremoniously from the arena and their meat distributed piecemeal to the poor or sold

COCKPIT *Cockfighting, though illegal in many places, is still widely practised.*

in the *plaza de toros;* that is, all but one bull – Gitanito.

Gitanito, meaning 'Little Gypsy', was the first bull in more than a decade to have walked free from the arena. In July 1993 he was pitted against top matador Damaso González in Valencia. He fought so bravely that it was accepted that he had matched the skill of the matador. 'Don't kill him,' shouted the crowd as they waved white handkerchiefs, the traditional sign that the bull should be spared. A cheer went up as the president of the *corrida* raised his handkerchief, too. The matador, for tradition's sake, faked a kill, plunging the sword into the sand. Gitanito would not fight again. Bulls, it seems, have remarkable memories and would not be as sporting a second time. Indeed, it is forbidden for a bull to be used twice. The animal would become too dangerous, having learned to go for the man rather than the cape. So Gitanito will spend the rest of his days at the stud farm.

The principle behind the bullfight (though there has been no scientific study) is based on a male herd animal's natural instinct to fight a rival or to attack something threatening him, his territory or his harem. By breeding for the most aggresive behaviour, the bulls are turned into entertainers. The same is true of camel-wrestling.

Each January in the ancient Roman stadium at Ephesus in Turkey, hybrid camels called *tulus* – a cross between Bactrian or two-humped camels and dromedaries or one-humped

AFTER THE FOX *A German fox hunt entertains the local gentry on St Hubert's Day (November 3).*

camels – fight. They cannot procreate but nevertheless show the same sexual aggression as breeding camels do during the rut. Using their powerful necks they crash into each other, trying to catch their opponent off balance. They bite their rival's legs and feet, often drawing blood. Today, the camels' mouths are gagged to avoid

BLOODSTAINED SPECTACULAR

In ancient Rome, thousands of animals were dispatched each year in dramatic pageants of killing. It was the fashionable entertainment of the time. On one fateful day, 50 000 spectators in the Coliseum paid to watch 230 assorted animals fighting and killing each other or killing armed and unarmed human martyrs. The animals were terrified by the noise of the crowd and, confronted by other wild and terror-stricken creatures they would have been unlikely to meet in the wild, they behaved with abnormal aggression. And the crowds loved it.

any serious damage, but in Roman times the camels would have fought until one was killed.

ONE MAN AND HIS DOG

Some animals provide entertainment as a by-product of their everyday life. Sheepdogs are working dogs, but their amazing ability to work closely with their shepherd

IN THE RING   A tiger riding on a rhino's back provides a spectacular circus act.

how the man–dog team performs. The shepherds guide their dogs with a series of commands and whistles, causing them to turn left or right, lie down or run. In effect, the shepherd is exploiting the hunting tactics of the ancestral wolf in separating a victim from the flock. Like wolves, the sheepdogs stalk and circle the flock, sometimes crouching if animals are alarmed, in order to control the direction in which the sheep are running.

The natural teamwork of a pack of dogs has been diverted into another entertainment: fox-hunting. This is probably a leftover from the days when foxes were a serious threat to livestock. Today, it

to drive sheep this way and that has become a spectator sport throughout the British Isles.

The dogs and their masters compete to collect small flocks of sheep, move them around obstacles and finally drive them into a pen, working against the clock and gathering points or faults depending on

is a diversion – though strongly disapproved of by many people – where the challenge is to outwit the wily, usually solitary, fox, using the hunting skills of a pack of hounds. The tradition is thought to have started in Europe in the 15th century, but it did not become a serious sport, with packs of hounds maintained exclusively for hunting, until the 17th century.

FOLLOWING THE HOUNDS

The hounds, usually 15 to 20 couples, behave much like a hunting wolf pack led not by a dominant dog but by a huntsman on horseback, aided by two or three 'whippers-in'. As with any social group, communication is important to keep order and in this case contact is maintained by sound – the huntsman's 'cheers' and the penetrating notes of the hunting horn. The

LOCAL HERO   A bullfighter in Ecuador is a champion pitting his wits against a 'wild' animal.

STAR TURNS — ANIMALS IN THE MOVIES

Some fortunate (or some might say, unfortunate) animals are particularly talented performers, and after considerable training end up on the stage, in films or on television. Dogs are particularly adept at performing. Their urge to please and their ability to appreciate visual and audible cues can be used to teach them quite complicated manoeuvres. Some have become stars in their own right.

Rin-Tin-Tin, a German shepherd dog, was brought back from the war in Europe by an American airman in 1918, and was trained to perform in dog shows in his new home of California. He was spotted by the movie moguls and went on to star in 40 films, earning more than $1 million, and helping to save the Warner Brothers film studios from going under. His natural ability to climb high walls, albeit with the help of hidden cleats, to run through walls of flame (his coat covered with fireproofing chemicals), to jump through panes of glass (made of sugar) and to show human-seeming expressions ranging from sadness to joy, made him a winner.

Lassie, the Yorkshire collie which starred in the film of Eric Knight's classic book *Lassie Come Home*, was originally called Pal. He went one better than 'Rinty' and barked, whined and growled on *The Lassie Radio Show*. One film reviewer remarked that Lassie was 'a Greer Garson in furs'.

Another animal superstar was Judy the chimpanzee, who featured in *Clarence the Cross-eyed Lion* and the spin-off television series *Daktari*. Judy learned more than 75 signals that indicated what she was supposed to do. There was even a signal for 'lunch'. Judy had such a good memory that when returning to the film set she would take up her position exactly as it had been before the break. Judy's costar, Clarence the lion, really was cross-eyed, and was so gentle that he allowed the chimpanzee to ride on his back.

And then there was Flipper. Flipper started out as 'Mitzi', a pet dolphin kept by a man who caught wild dolphins for marine circuses and aquariums. She became the first trained dolphin to work with people in the water. She was taught to fetch a ball and then learned to bring back the trainer's nine-year-old son, who eventually rode on her back.

But not all rising stars were as successful as Lassie, Judy and Flipper. When making the movie *Tarzan's Greatest Adventure* in 1959, two trained chimpanzees who were to take turns playing Tarzan's faithful friend Cheetah were shipped from Britain to Kenya. The animals were so terrified of the sounds from the bush that only one featured briefly in the film as Tarzan uttered the words 'So long, Cheetah.'

HOLLYWOOD STAR *A lion with a host of unlikely companions features in the movie* Tarzan and the Valley of Gold.

hunt starts when the master moves the hounds off to 'draw' (search) a covert, a patch of woodland or a field in which a fox is thought to be hiding. The hounds cry out when the quarry is found and the call of 'tallyho' encourages the human participants on horseback to follow the pursuing hounds. When the fox is seen, a high-pitched cry – the 'holloa' – is given and the hounds jostle in for the kill. The fox is dispatched and the master gives the 'brush' (tail), 'mask' (head) and 'pads' (feet) to followers he considers worthy of the honour. The remains of the fox's body are thrown to the dogs. As often as not, the fox outmanoeuvres the pack and gets away.

Activities like this, where the natural abilities of a wary quarry provide sport for human beings, have long been common throughout the world. Stag-hunting and otter-hunting with packs of specially bred hounds provide similar 'entertainment'. Another blood sport involving dogs is hare-coursing, using 'sight' or gaze hounds, such as Afghans, salukis and greyhounds – among the earliest forms of hunting dogs. In centuries gone by, the Persians hunted gazelles with salukis for sport, and the Russian nobility used packs of borzois (Russian wolfhounds) to hunt wolves – hunting like with like.

Another 'entertainment' with ancient origins in the Middle and Far East is cock-fighting. Gamecocks are bred to fight in circular arenas or 'pits' about 20 ft (6 m) across, with enthusiastic spectators placing bets. The birds are pitted against each other, the punters relying on the cocks to follow their natural tendency to attack another of the same species.

PLACE YOUR BETS

The fighting cock, like the domestic chicken, is probably descended from the Indian red jungle fowl. The males of this species have a spur on the back of each heel, but in the fighting pit artificial spurs enhance the effectiveness of these natural weapons: they are made of bone or metal and may be over 2 in (5 cm) long. At the start of a fight, the birds square up to each other and then attack – feet, claws and spurs first. Originally, cocks fought for the right to mate with the hens, and this instinct is deliberately cultivated in fighting cocks by breeding with the most aggressive birds.

Placing the birds in an enclosure with no escape route also has its effect. In the birds' natural environment, a repertoire of

gestures, postures, calls and other safety valves would be used to avoid fighting. Physical confrontation is often the last resort, when two equally matched rivals can find no other way in which to settle the contest. Birds in the fighting pit, however, have no choice. Neither can back off, and so they fight, sometimes to the death or at least until one contestant cannot carry on. Modern practice is to remove a damaged bird before the fight goes too far, but in

some parts of the world cockfights still include the 'battle royal', in which several birds are set in the pit and they fight until just one survives.

Wagers on animals that are forced to fight are not confined to aggressive chickens. In some countries, dogs, such as pit-bull terriers, are bred for their aggressiveness and placed in the fighting pit. Even more brutal, in the past, was bear-baiting, when chained bears were attacked by packs of dogs in theatre-like arenas called 'bear gardens'. Proceedings were livened up by blowing pepper into the bear's nose.

In parts of South-east Asia, bull buffaloes are encouraged to come head to head in an exciting contest that can spill over into the audience. And in the Alps, specially bred cows (not bulls) are let loose in fields where they fight it out. The cows have large numbers painted on their sides for easy recognition and farmers bet on the result.

Less cruel, but nevertheless exciting, is the habit of betting on animals' natural athleticism. This happens in many kinds of races, with creatures as varied as frogs, snails, beetles, camels, greyhounds and, of course, thoroughbred racehorses.

HORSE SENSE

Horses, of all the racing animals, probably have the greatest stamina. In the wild, they can run at top speed over rough terrain for hours on end. They need to do so to escape, for horses are fundamentally animals that are preyed on rather than preying. They have the mental wherewithal to spot predators and the physical strength to flee from them. Horses are understandably wary. A predator can afford to make a mistake and live to chase again another day, but for a wild horse a mistake can be fatal. As a result, domestic horses can seem irrationally nervous, taking fright, for example, at the sight of a piece of white paper in the hedgerow. This does not mean the horse is

IN THE WHALE'S MOUTH *An act with an orca or killer whale and a female trainer is the seaquarium's equivalent of 'putting your head in the lion's mouth'.*

CREATURES IN CAPTIVITY: THE LURE OF THE ZOO

One convenient way to view exotic wild animals without travelling across the world to see them in their natural habitats, is to visit a zoo or wildlife park. The origins of zoos lie in the distant past. In 1150 BC, the Chinese Empress Tanki established a marble house in which to keep deer, and around 1000 BC King Solomon was a noted zookeeper. Today, zoos and safari parks are popular with the

PREVENTIVE MEASURES
African lions breed so well in zoos that they have to be supplied with contraceptives.

general public, though frowned upon by some people who feel that zoos are no more than prisons. Whatever the case, it is clear that some animals actually do well in zoos, their natural behaviour affected little by their confinement.

Lions, for example, are basically lazy animals. In the wild they sit or lie around most of the day, only moving

PROWLING TIGERS *Tigers pace up and down almost automatically, their feet falling in exactly the same place each time they cross the cage.*

to procure a meal. If they can scavenge a dead carcass or steal another predator's prey, rather than catch their own food, they will do so. In zoos, lions have taken to the easy life of captivity so readily that they have become prolific breeders. Most lionesses in zoos are now given contraceptives to reduce their numbers. Polar bears, on the other hand, do not look comfortable. They are Arctic wanderers and in zoos show signs of abnormal behaviour: strange, repetitive head and neck movements, continuous pacing up and down, and chewing objects such as plastic bowls.

Many species, including some of the larger animals – the rhinos and giraffes, for example – settle down well at safari parks, where they have space to roam almost freely, but space is not always the problem; boredom is a greater quandary, particularly for primates. Zoos have tackled this by presenting animals such as the more intelligent monkeys

and apes with problems to solve and tasks to complete.

The basic problem for most zoo animals is that their food is provided for them. Foraging time for a zoo animal is idle time. So zoos now

YEARNING FOR FREEDOM
Polar bears rarely thrive in zoos, where they make strange, neurotic movements.

make animals work for their dinner. Chimpanzees, for example, have been taught to 'fish' with grass stems for termites, honey or other foods from artificial termite nests. Peccaries – piglike animals from the Americas – which find their food under leaf litter, have their zoo food buried under bark and sand so that they must sniff it out and dig it up.

The zoos of today are trying to create conditions in which a zoo animal might have a chance to behave in a manner similar to its free-living relatives in the wild.

not intelligent – its intellect is that of a natural prey and something white in a sea of browns and greens is unusual enough to warrant caution.

In fact, horses have shown high intelligence. They do well in discrimination tests, where they are able to distinguish circles, squares, dots, semicircles and triangles; they also have long memories. In one experiment, horses were trained to discriminate among shapes and they consistently scored between 70 and 100 per cent in subsequent tests. Remarkably, a year later, without further training, they achieved the same scores.

These equine talents have been harnessed for entertainment in the circus and in some 'high school' or *haute école* riding establishments, such as the Imperial Spanish Riding School of Vienna, as well as in the show-jumping arena and on the eventing course. Here, the abilities of the horse are often combined with those of a human rider, so that horse and rider perform as one. They communicate by a recognised series of movements, passed from the rider's hands through the reins and bit to the horse's mouth, or when riders press their legs and heels against the horse's body. Horses remember these instructions by repetition. But no matter how skilled the rider, many showjumpers admit to occasions when their horse seemed to sense that they were not quite together during a round – the horse literally carried them over the jumps and around the course.

MARINE CIRCUS

One of the most talented performers from the animal world is the bottle-nosed dolphin. Dolphins, with their permanent

CAT LOVE *According to polls, cats rather than dogs are the most popular pets in Europe and North America.*

smiles, seem to revel in doing tricks for a paying audience. They jump out of the water in formation, play basketball, swim upside down, jump through flaming hoops and walk on their tails – all for the reward of a piece of fish. Many of the tricks mimic natural behaviour in the wild: 'spy-hopping' to observe what is happening on the surface and making noises to keep in touch with other members of the school. Dolphin trainers simply extend those natural skills and adapt them to create stunts.

Interestingly, dolphins asked to do the same trick over and over again will eventually get bored, refuse to cooperate and sulk. They continually need new stimuli. In this they resemble people. Most animals lose the play instinct when they grow up, having equipped themselves during adolescence for the niche they will fill. Only two animals never grow up – humans and dolphins. Both retain an innate inquisitiveness and continue to find out about the world.

PETS AND PEOPLE

People keep pets for a variety of reasons. Many humans talk to and seek affection from pets, whether cats, dogs, parrots, budgerigars, hamsters, rabbits or white mice, and there is evidence that the animals listen and respond to the utterances people make, even if they do not fully appreciate what is being said.

People often think the animals understand. Indeed, in a survey it was found that

INHERITED FRIENDLINESS

Over half the households in Europe and North America have at least one pet. Cats, of which there are 5 million in Britain alone, are the most popular – owners apparently enjoy their haughty, independent attitude. Some cats are friendlier than others, and particularly friendly ones often have the same father – leading researchers to believe that there is an inherited factor. This need not be a specific gene for friendliness, but some influence, say, on the cat's growth rate that enables it to be more confident and therefore more friendly.

nine out of ten pet owners believed that their pets understood their moods. But do pets really know how their owners are feeling or comprehend what they are saying? And can they perceive by a mind-reading process people's unspoken thoughts?

There are other explanations. A move towards the dog's leash will tell any perceptive canine that it is time for a walk, and dogs are capable of picking up much more subtle cues. Most animals, for instance, have a remarkable appreciation of the passage of time. The move to put on a coat before a walk at the same time each evening is easily anticipated by the animal. To the uninitiated, it appears that the dog has read the person's mind. In reality, its internal clock has simply told it that the time has come for that particular activity.

In nature there are some amazing feats of timing, like the honeybee that flies to a particular species of flower at certain times of the day to coincide its visit with the periodic production of nectar. In zoos, animals pace their cages and look beseechingly towards the zookeeper's hut as dinner time approaches. In the wild this instinct is a survival mechanism. It ensures, for example, that day-adapted creatures are out of harm's way before the night shift arrives.

As for the clairvoyant pet, there may be

IN THE COLD *Dogs can be household pets or active working animals like the husky.*

even more hidden cues. Animals' senses are much more acute than humans' are. Like any other animals, humans emit radiations, ranging from heat to the electrical activity of their muscles. These may reflect changes in people's physical and emotional states that can be detected by a pet. Simply anticipating a walk may result in a subtle signal that the pet picks up. Again, it is a survival mechanism – the alertness needed by any animal. The pet is ready to react immediately to something that is about to happen.

Then there is body language – the unconscious changes or movements of the body that transmit messages that other humans and pets are able to pick up. In one series of experiments, it was noticed that if people are interested in something, the pupils in their eyes become larger, whereas if they are looking at something distasteful or uninteresting they contract. The culmination of the experiments came when male subjects were presented with two pictures of an attractive woman. In one her pupils were touched up to look larger. The men were asked to indicate which picture they preferred. Most said they could see no difference, but their eyes gave them away. The pupil size of the men was monitored during the experiment, and it was found their pupils widened too in response to the woman's wide-eyed look. They had unconsciously recognised that her eyes were saying 'I'm interested in you'.

The pupils in a cat's eyes also enlarge and contract, so that when it is presented with something it likes the pupils dilate. Confusingly, the pupils also enlarge in response to something frightening. It is as if the animal has been stimulated to such an extent, by pleasure or fear, that it needs to obtain more visual information. Humans, however, can lie by putting out contradictory signals. People can be saying 'I am calm' while their body language, such as sweating palms, shows that they are far from calm. Some hunters, such as cheetahs and baboons, also do this. They saunter along showing no interest in the victim, but their apparent nonchalance hides alertness: when they are close enough, they take off and attack. The ability to read body language is another strategy for survival.

MAKING CONTACT

An animal's ability to 'talk' using gestures or symbols and work out puzzles has long fascinated humans. Scientists are trying to measure this ability and establish how intelligent animals really are.

The Minotaur, according to Greek legend, was confined to a labyrinth or maze – an intricate network of paths designed to mislead and confuse anybody or anything entering it by frequent changes of direction and blind turnings.

This mythological beast, half man and half bull, was intelligent enough to find its way around its convoluted world in order to devour the seven Athenian youths and seven maidens who were sent into the labyrinth each year (or every ninth year according to some accounts). The labyrinth was thus a test site for humans. Gods, with their superhuman intelligence, had no trouble in finding their way in and out, but mortals were not so clever. The maze sorted out the bright from the not so bright – as it still does in the behavioural research laboratories of the world. Today, it is research scientists – ethologists, who study animal behaviour – who use the maze as one of their tools.

Ants can find their way around laboratory mazes, as can pigeons, rabbits, rats, mice, lemon sharks and many more creatures. Their ability to do so and the time they take to do it is a reflection of their ability to remember, reflect and perhaps to reason. It turns out that some of them are particularly adept at finding their way. One of the most interesting maze experiments was devised by the scientist David Olton to measure animal memory. He created an eight-armed maze with transparent tunnels

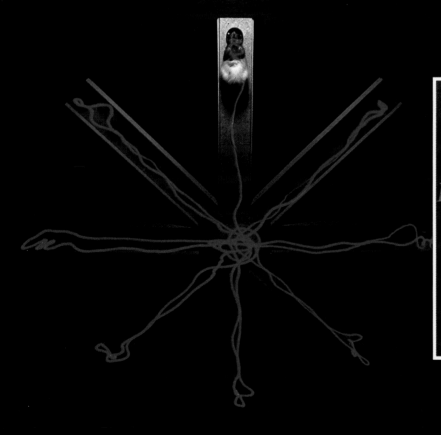

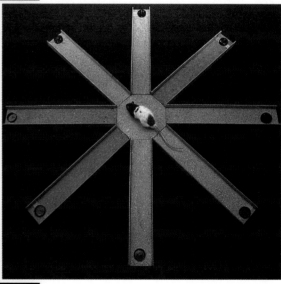

SPEEDY LEARNERS *Rats soon learn how to locate food in an eight-armed maze without visiting the same arm twice.*

green disc, and after a while the bird learned to peck mainly when it saw green. Making the test slightly more complicated, the experimenters released food only after the passage of a set length of time – say a minute between rewards. Eventually, the pigeon learned that pecking just after it had received a reward, even when the disc was green, was fruitless, but as the minute ended, its rate of pecking increased.

SPOT THE DIFFERENCE

Animals also remember what they have seen. In an experiment at the University of Texas, monkeys were shown pairs of photographs and taught to press one of two buttons representing 'same' and 'different'. They could spot the relevant pictures even when 20 or more different photographs separated the two similar pictures.

In another test, at Harvard University, pigeons were taught to discriminate among objects. Using the Skinner box, pigeons were shown colour photographs but they were only rewarded when there were trees in the picture, which they responded to by pecking a disc. The pigeons learned to distinguish trees from lampposts, vines growing over walls, telephone poles, a stick of celery and other tree-like

emerging from a centre like the spokes of a wheel. Each tunnel diverged from its neighbour by 45°. At the end of the tunnels he placed a scrap of food. His subject was a hungry laboratory rat.

Not surprisingly, the rat quickly found the food pellets, but what was unusual about the result of this experiment was the way in which the rat performed. After it had settled down, it learned how to empty the maze without going down the same tunnel twice. It did not follow a set pattern: one time it went down the tunnel numbered 7, then 8, then 4, 1, 5, 3, 6, 2, and another time it followed the sequence 4-2-3-7-5-1-8-6. The route it took could not be predicted. So how did it know which arms it had visited and which it had not?

One suggestion was that it left an odour marker at the entrance to each tunnel it had entered, but the researcher conducting the experiment eliminated that possibility. The clue came when the maze was rotated through 90°. It turned out that the rat used visual landmarks that it picked up from outside the maze – some tunnels were near a window, others under an electric light – so when the maze was moved the rat became disorientated: it entered

tunnels that it had already been down because their position in relation to the objects in the laboratory had changed. The test demonstrated that the rat could 'picture' the location of the tunnels it had already entered. In so doing it was able to reflect on its recent experience in order to find food with the minimum of effort.

Pigeons have given even more impressive performances. The pigeon is not presented with a maze but instead is placed in a 'Skinner box'. It works on the same principle as a vending machine, only instead of inserting money to get food, the pigeon must peck on a disc. Then it receives a reward from a food hopper. In this way pigeons have been taught to respond to quite complex problems.

In a relatively simple test, the colour of the disc alternated unpredictably between green and blue. Food was released only when the pigeon saw a

items. This was repeated with water, including bodies of water, snow and raindrops, and with fish, including eels, flatfish, sharks and tropical fish. The birds could even discriminate among animals such as turtles, whales and dolphins. This was all the more remarkable since pigeons see trees and water in the natural world, but they rarely if ever meet fish.

The pigeons could also recognise individual human faces and the expressions on them. Photographs of four people – two male and two female of about the same age, two of them fair-haired, the other two dark-haired – were shown to the pigeons. Each photograph also featured one of four emotions: happiness with broad grins; anger with threatening scowls; surprise with open mouths and staring eyes; and disgust with twisted lips. After a period of learning the pigeons passed their test; they were even able to observe the expression on one face and recognise it on another. In distinguishing water, trees, fish and faces, the birds had shown that they were able to learn and appreciate 'concepts'.

In the wild, this ability was observed in plovers. In a field experiment, two men walked close to a plovers' nest. One man was wearing a red anorak and the other a blue one. The man in red hovered menacingly close to the nest, whereas the one in blue passed by without stopping. Some time later the two men walked past the nest again. As the one in blue came close to the nest the birds all but ignored him, but as the man in red approached, the birds became agitated and began to perform their characteristic 'broken wing' display to try to lure him away. The birds had learned which of the people was the greater threat.

SIGN LANGUAGE

Getting animals to tell us what they see and how they feel is not easy. After all, humans do not all utter the same kinds of sounds or speak the same language. But researchers

GIVE US A DRINK *A chimp asks for a drink using hand signals based on the American Sign Language for the Deaf.*

have long thought how convenient it would be if they could communicate directly with representatives of other species. From the early days of research in the late 19th century until as late as the 1960s, experimenters tried to teach monkeys, apes and dolphins to speak English, but failed. Even humankind's closest relatives do not have the physical capability to form words. But they do have hands. Why not make use of ape and human dexterity to create a new language that both might use?

Sign languages of one sort or another have been used for thousands of years. It is likely that a gestural language was used by early man, particularly out hunting when sounds would have alerted the prey. The Plains Indians of North America have a well-documented sign language, and the Bushmen of the Kalahari and Australian Aborigines have specific gestures by which they can communicate at times when making a sound is inappropriate or inconvenient. Today bookmakers have their tick-tack language and referees and umpires in basketball, baseball and cricket have their visual signals. And there is another useful sign language – that of the deaf.

In the 1920s, the American primatologist R.M. Yerkes wrote: 'I am inclined to conclude from the various evidences that the great apes have plenty to talk about, but no gift for the use of sounds . . . Perhaps they can be taught to use their fingers, somewhat as does the deaf and dumb person, and helped to acquire a simple, nonvocal sign language.'

Forty years later, Allen and Beatrice Gardner, working at the University of Nevada, took up Yerkes's challenge and began a series of experiments with a chimpanzee who was to become one of the most famous of her kind. Her name was Washoe, and she became the first chimp to

LIFE AND DEATH WITH KOKO THE GORILLA

Researcher Penny Patterson met Koko, a one-year-old gorilla, at San Francisco Zoo in 1972 and since then the two have rarely been parted. Koko, like other apes, has been taught sign language for the deaf and has come up with some remarkable inventions.

One of his first creations was when a woodpecker was drumming nearby. Koko's teacher signed 'Koko, listen bird'. Koko held the sign for 'bird', looked into his teacher's eyes and raised his eyebrows. With this gesture he had turned a statement into a question. Then, having established that he understood, he gave the woodpecker its gorilla-style name, 'listen bird'.

Koko also played tricks on his teacher. Once he was asked to sign 'drink' and used every appropriate word he knew, from 'sip' to 'thirsty-sip' to 'apple-sip', but stubbornly refused to sign 'drink'. The exhausted and exasperated teacher eventually pleaded with Koko, and the gorilla sat back with a grin on his face and signed a perfect 'drink', but as if pouring the drink into his ear.

On another occasion, Koko was asked about death. The conversation went as follows:

Teacher:	*Where do gorillas go when they die?*
Koko:	*Comfortable hole, bye.*
Teacher:	*When do gorillas die?*
Koko:	*Trouble old. And tigers.*
Teacher:	*Don't like tigers?*
Koko:	*Frown bad red.*
Teacher:	*I like tigers.*
Koko:	*Tiger nail rough.*

Teacher:	*What animals do you like?*
Koko:	*Gorilla love.*

That gorillas and chimpanzees are able to use a sign language is not too surprising. In the wild, they live in social groups that stay together over the long term and they must be able to 'think ahead' in order to resolve the conflicting pressures of competition and cooperation that exist in such groups.

Indeed, apes have their own 'languages' of gestures and grunts that are important in a close social group. It could be this social need that enables gorillas and chimps to do things in an environment where language is used a lot which they would never do in the wild, such as speaking with a sign language.

be taught a human gestural language – American Sign Language or ASL.

Washoe was brought up to learn ASL, and all the other members of the research team had to do so, too. Only ASL was used in the chimp's presence. Sounds were only allowed as spontaneous expressions of joy

LIMITED ENGLISH

Before using sign language, researchers tried to teach apes the spoken word. One orang-utan featured in tests in 1909. Physician William Furness manipulated the mouth, lips and tongue of the animal, which could eventually say 'papa' and 'cup'. In the 1940s, chimpanzee Viki in Florida learned to say 'mama', 'papa', 'cup' and 'up'. Her nose was blocked so the sounds came through the mouth. Humans do this by raising the palate to block off the nasal chamber. Chimps cannot do this and failed to impress anyone with their limited English.

or surprise. Within four years she had learned 130 signs and was able to put them together with considerable inventiveness.

Signs were created for every event or

task that was performed in the course of a normal day. Washoe remembered them simply by seeing them regularly. She slowly learned to associate specific signs with particular objects or activities. She disliked, for example, cleaning her teeth, but after each meal was encouraged to do so. The sign was simply to move the index finger across her teeth. Imagine, then, the surprise when Washoe visited the Gardners' house, went to the bathroom, climbed onto the basin and, sitting beside a rack filled with the Gardners' toothbrushes, made the sign for 'teeth cleaning'. Washoe certainly had no intention of cleaning her teeth but, much like a stranger at a cocktail party seizing on a familiar topic, had simply wanted to strike up a conversation.

The more she learned, the more specific the meaning of her signs became. At first when Washoe was attracted to a smell she would make the sign for 'flower'. Gradually, she distinguished cooking smells from flower smells, and her 'flower' sign was used for flowers, indoors and out, real or painted. She had shown that she had recognised things for what they were, rather than associating them only with objects employed in the experiments.

Later she began to combine words, linking the sign for 'open' with other words, such as 'open food drink' on approaching the refrigerator. She also told of her future intentions with signs for 'go in', 'go out' and 'in down bed'. Even more interestingly she differentiated between 'I me' and 'you'. Washoe was conscious of herself and said so, and in doing so contributed, albeit in a simple way, to the philosophical debate taxing the great minds in the human world on the concept of 'self'.

Washoe was also tested to help to prove or disprove that she was actually using the sign language and not just copying. She

did tolerably well at identifying colour photographs and models in a box, but more interesting were the answers that she got wrong, for although incorrect, they were conceptually significant. She signed 'dog' when the picture was of a cat, 'brush' for comb, and 'food' for meat. Her response to real and toy objects was also significant. Washoe's response to a plastic toy dog was to sign 'baby'. She also signed 'baby' to a picture of a toy dog, but to a picture of a real dog she signed 'dog'.

As a whole, the observations were intriguing, sometimes surprising, and often amusing, but their significance was often questioned by researchers in the field. Was Washoe really using language? The Gardners were cautious. It was clear that Washoe had a preference for the order of

words in her simple 'sentences'. The signs for 'you-me' took precedence over 'me-you', and in three-word combinations, she preferred 'you-action-me'. Was this evidence of syntax or simply an imitation of a preferred word order introduced by a member of the research team?

Whatever the answer, some researchers believe that there is little difference between the way in which Washoe selected her order of words and the way human children learn syntax. In one exchange, the similarity between the chimp talking to her trainer and a child talking to its mother was marked. The conversation in sign language went like this:

Washoe: *Gimme.*
Trainer: *What this?* (that is, *What do you want?*)
Washoe: *Food. Gimme.*
Trainer: *Ask politely.*
Washoe: *Please.*

Washoe was the first ape to use sign language, but many others followed. Like children, they learned at different rates and were good at different things. One young female chimp with a depressingly low score would do well if showered with praise. In double-blind trials, in which her trainers were also prevented from seeing the nature of the task set for her, she failed. There were, however, more stars like Washoe.

Lucy was another chimpanzee sign-linguist. She became well known for her original sign-language descriptions of fruits and vegetables. Watermelons were signed as 'candy drink' or sometimes 'drink fruit'. Citrus fruits became 'smell fruits'. Another example was her encounter with a radish. At first she examined the little vegetable carefully and signed 'fruit food'. She was, however, reluctant to eat it. After a while she took the plunge and took a bite, immediately spitting it out and signing 'cry hurt food'. This novel combination of sign-language words showed that Lucy could use her existing vocabulary to create new concepts that encapsulated

LANGUAGE KEYS *Touching symbols on a keyboard helps a chimp to communicate with humans.*

THE IMPORTANCE OF MAKING HAND SIGNALS

Researchers into ape language and hand signing are often criticised for making their findings fit in with human patterns. The animals are learning an artificial language, say some scholars, using their hands in a way that is unnatural to them. New research by David Perrett of St Andrews University in Scotland, however, suggests that human beings' own ancestors used their hands in gestures and mime before they used the spoken word. Sign language is apparently a natural way to communicate for many primates.

The research at St Andrews has been with macaque monkeys, and has shown that there are regions in the brain that respond to the sight of hand shapes. In fact, the monkeys' brains are programmed to recognise hand shapes – shapes that are not

Hand Dialogue Gestures used in the wild are similar to those in the sign language for the deaf taught in captivity (right). Arm-stretch movements are part of a dialogue between chimpanzee brothers (below).

Facing It Out Two male chimpanzees confront one another with hand movements and similar gestures.

dissimilar to those used in sign language for the deaf. This is the same signing that is used in ape-language experiments.

Similarly, the macaque's brain is also genetically programmed to respond to particular ways in which the faces of other monkeys and apes are presented to it. As the brain has been set up by evolution to attend to the things and events important to its survival, it follows that the shapes and gestures displayed by hands and faces are important in the life of

monkeys or apes, including humans.

Humankind's early ancestors, for example, would probably have used signs and gestures when hunting cooperatively. Instead of shouting

'There's an antelope over there' and scaring the animal away, they would have made a sign, using the hands to indicate the nature and direction of the potential source of food.

her understanding of the objects presented to her. She was, in effect, demonstrating an ability to think in the abstract.

Washoe, meanwhile, trained some young chimps herself. She taught ASL to a foster chimp called Loulis. The keepers

were careful to use only five signs in front of Loulis, so the rest of her vocabulary must have come from Washoe. Washoe was using the artificial sign language not only to communicate with humans but also to talk to another member of her own species.

It is not practical to try to teach a chimp to write with a pen or pencil, but it can be taught to use computers – where it only has to press keys – and plastic tokens to exchange messages. At the University of Pennsylvania, David and Ann Premack

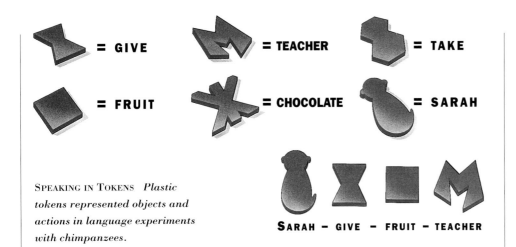

= GIVE

= FRUIT

= TEACHER

= CHOCOLATE

= TAKE

= SARAH

SARAH – GIVE – FRUIT – TEACHER

SPEAKING IN TOKENS *Plastic tokens represented objects and actions in language experiments with chimpanzees.*

looked after Sarah, a six-year-old chimp who used plastic tokens to represent words. In effect, Sarah was using a form of writing – not with a pen, but with pieces of plastic.

Sarah's training was laborious. She was introduced to an object and then by a series of simple steps began to associate it with a piece of coloured plastic. She was given an apple, for example, and first allowed to eat it. Then she had to learn that to receive another she must use the correct token, in the apple's case a blue triangle. Each of her trainers was also represented by a token, and Sarah was taught that a particular token represented herself.

Having acquired some nouns, Sarah was introduced to verbs, such as 'give'. To win a fruit reward she had to use 'give' and, for instance, the trainer's name, thereby building up simple combinations of words. Eventually she went on to use more complicated sentences. With a bribe of chocolate she could be made to part with a piece of fruit with the word combination 'Sarah-give-fruit-teacher'. Sarah used a 130-word vocabulary and secured a miscellany of linguistic skills. Her performance, it was thought, compared favourably with the language abilities of a two-year-old child.

NIM CHIMPSKY

Since Washoe's and Sarah's pioneering experiments, there have been many clever chimps working with tools, including specialised computer keyboards, synthesised voices and so on. But one series of experiments carried out with a chimp called Nim at Columbia University, New York, was to pour cold water on the achievements of the 'talking' apes. Nim, like the others, acquired a large sign-language vocabulary but when researchers analysed their videotapes they discovered that about 90 per cent of conversations were initiated by the trainer not by Nim.

It was felt that a child would have started up a far higher proportion of conversations. A child imitates its parents less and less as it gets older. At 21 months, a child copies about 20 per cent of its parents' utterances but at three years it has stopped direct copying altogether. Nim, however, imitated his teachers 38 per cent of the time aged 26 months and increased his copying to 54 per cent at just over three years old. Although his vocabulary increased, his word combinations did not. Children tend to expand on what they have learned from their parents and their sentences become longer and more structured. Nim did not do that.

In short, the researchers felt that Nim's signing was simply an irritating and meaningless way to gain a reward at the end of the session. It is illustrated by his signing of 'cat' to get to play with his pet cat. The sign

had little more function than to get the cat. He did not ask 'Where is the cat?' or say 'There is a white cat over there'. During the supposed conversation, all he did was imitate his teacher and throw in a few extra words that, to the human, looked grammatically interesting. In effect Nim was making a demand, not exchanging information or holding a conversation.

Shock waves reverberated throughout the scientific community and it showed how difficult it is to interpret what we see. There is a human analogy that illustrates the problem. An English schoolboy is on holiday in France but knows no French. Children do not need language to join in games and so it comes as no surprise when his father finds him playing football with the local boys. But he is very impressed when the boy, spotting a gap in the opposing team's defences, shouts '*Ici, ici!*', and the ball is passed to him and he scores a goal. After the game has finished the father asks his son what *ici* means.

'I really don't know,' the boy replies, 'but every time I shout it, I get the ball.'

The boy has mimicked the other boys, used the right word, and achieved what he wanted, but he has no idea what it means.

GORILLASPEAK *Gorillas, like this TV addict, and other great apes are able to talk using sign language.*

KANZI: THE 'TALKING' CHIMP

Kanzi is a special kind of chimpanzee in all sorts of ways. He is a bonobo or pygmy chimpanzee, a species that split from common chimpanzee stock about 5 million years ago. Bonobo and common chimps are remarkable in that they share all but 1 per cent of their genetic make-up with humans.

Kanzi, like all bonobos, looks intelligent and he certainly behaves in an extremely sophisticated way. He has taken the study of ape language and of human-animal communications into a new sphere. For one thing, he appears to understand spoken English and can 'speak' back by

SCHOOL IN THE FOREST *Lessons continue in the large forest of the Language Research Center, Georgia, where Kanzi played freely when he was young.*

pressing brightly coloured geometric symbols, known as lexigrams, on a special keyboard. His mentor, the leading ape-language researcher Sue Savage-Rumbaugh at Georgia State University in the United States, can then hear what he has to say through an artificial 'voice' that articulates the words that Kanzi selects.

An even more extraordinary fact is that Kanzi was not at first the focus of the language researchers' attentions. It was his adoptive mother, Matata, who was really being taught the symbols, meanings and contexts of their language system; Kanzi just picked them up by himself, without prompting.

After Matata, who had been born in the wild, failed to learn half a dozen of the

KANZI SPEAKING *Kanzi understands spoken English but replies with symbols. In his laboratory, he 'talks' to children.*

256 available lexigrams, Kanzi – just 2½ years old – pressed the symbol for 'chase'. He looked imploringly at the attendant

scientist and scampered playfully away. After that, there was no holding him. Choosing his own lexigram 'words' for a variety of objects and actions, Kanzi used his keyboard to request food, to initiate favourite play activities and to announce what he was going to do next. Even more astonishing was that he seemed to be able to put 'meaning' into his messages. If his mother initiated an action – biting, say – he would signal 'Matata bite', but if she was on the receiving end Kanzi would signal 'bite Matata'.

The order of words and actions was also important. If Kanzi wanted to be chased and then play-bitten – the bonobo's equivalent of tickling – he would sign the lexigrams in that order. If the researchers tried to reverse the sequence, Kanzi would have none of it and refused to be play-bitten until he had first been chased.

Sometimes Kanzi used the keyboard in combination with hand gestures, but again he invented his own 'linguistic' rules. The lexigram always preceded the gesture. So, if he wanted to visit one of the research centre's pet dogs he first pressed the symbol for 'dog' and then gestured 'go'.

By doing these things Kanzi had unwittingly refuelled the ape-language

AT THE KEYBOARD *Kanzi and his instructor Sue Savage-Rumbaugh sit at a lexigram keyboard. This contains the symbols he uses to communicate with people.*

debate. He had demonstrated not only that a bonobo can learn simple grammar but also that it can invent new rules – rules that had not been demonstrated to it by a human. Furthermore, the researchers had tried to eliminate the 'mimic' factor and scotch the critics by recording only data that showed the chimpanzee using symbols on his own: he could not be accused of merely mimicking his human mentors.

One more recent achievement was suggested by Nicholas Roth from Indiana University, a scientist interested in the links between the evolution of tool use and that of language. He showed Kanzi how to make stone tools. The researchers now watch with interest to see if Kanzi will teach the technique to other chimpanzees and create a community of toolmakers. This may provide a window through which we can observe behaviour that is similar to that of our early hominid (manlike) ancestors.

ABLE TO TALK *Kanzi's communication abilities suggest that some apes have the brain power for a primitive language.*

Indeed, some researchers now believe that chimpanzees like Kanzi, with a brain one-third the size of a human's, are likely to have much the same abilities as early hominids. Not only might Kanzi hold the key to the origins and evolution of human language, he might also encourage us to examine our attitudes towards our nearest animal relatives – they are, after all, turning out to be more like us than we once dared to believe. Kanzi has in a way broken down the barrier between apes and people. Humans, it can now be argued, share a branch of the tree of life with chimpanzees and gorillas, rather than being in a distinct and separate line of their own.

Such a shift in classification raises many questions. Should these close relatives have some kind of legal status, perhaps the same as that granted to young human children? Should the higher apes be kept in zoos? Kanzi's outstanding communication skills may lead people into taking a second look at the way in which we view not only the great apes but also all other animals.

ACTIVITIES OF THE MIND

The sperm whale has the largest brain of any creature, but it is not the most intelligent. A brain has to be big and complex enough to provide an animal with the mental capacity it needs to survive.

The Swiss zoologist Heini Hediger referred to 'the age-old burning desire of mankind to take up language contact with other animals'. He made the comment during a conference of linguists, psychologists, philosophers and biologists, many of whom were working in the field of human-animal communication.

Wanting to make contact is not a frivolous venture. There is, after all, the view, held by some philosophers, that language comes before thought. Without language there can be no thinking. Therefore if animals do think, they must have some linguistic means of doing so. As with humans, therefore, access to an animal's mind must be through language, and this has been approached in two ways.

The first way is to study the animals in the wild. Research workers in the field have tried to understand an animal's natural gestures, postures and sounds. Whether the animal is using a 'language' is debatable, but it is certainly telling its tale in its own 'words'. The problem for the researcher is that in interpreting the observations it is easy to anthropomorphise – that is, see things in human terms.

The second way of studying animal communications happens in much more controlled conditions. Researchers in the laboratory have tried to teach animals man-made languages. But this poses some fundamental problems of usage and interpretation. We know what we mean when using specific signs in a particular order, but do we really know what an animal means or if it understands anything at all?

Both ways of investigation are open to some misinterpretation. When trying to communicate with, or comprehend the ways of, another animal, humans have little understanding of the nature or context of its behaviour. Animals may view the world very differently from the way in which humans do. As a result, our observations thus far may be giving us not so much a view of the intelligence of other creatures as a reflection of ourselves.

Scientists can take a leaf out of the books of magicians and illusionists whose tricks depend on the way in which people are hoodwinked by suggestions and expectation. Examples include a favourite old circus trick known as 'The Kiss of Death' in which a scantily clad girl is strapped to a bed. A large bear is released and it heads straight for the girl. The audience is concerned for the girl, expecting to witness an attack. Instead the bear appears to kiss the girl and then it shuffles back to its cage. The bear's thoughts, unlike those of

MEETING OF MINDS *Two apes – a mountain gorilla and a human – contemplate their nearness.*

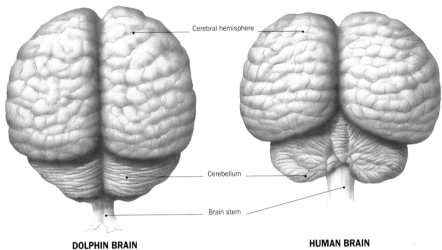

Cerebral hemisphere

Cerebellum

Brain stem

DOLPHIN BRAIN   **HUMAN BRAIN**

HUMAN VS DOLPHIN *The dolphin's brain is larger than the human's, but has a thinner neocortex, the part with which we create, innovate and reason.*

the audience, were not of attack, but on the piece of carrot hidden in the girl's mouth.

In Britain, a study of the behaviour of police dogs also illustrated the way in which people can easily be misled. The police dog is supposed to be able to follow a scent trail and in this way to lead its handler to the target. But in one study researchers discovered that the handler was giving the dog subtle cues to his own expectations about the route they should follow. The handler had unwittingly steered the dog in the direction he thought they should go. The dog was not leading the man; the man was leading the dog.

TESTING BRAIN SIZE

Given the pitfalls of misinterpretation and anthropomorphism, are there any animals that can definitely be said to show great intelligence? Which creatures are likely to have the brain capacity and the motivation to learn? Candidates include our nearest relatives – the chimpanzee and gorilla – and our best friends – the dog and the cat. Another possibility is the seemingly highly intelligent invertebrate, the octopus. Some researchers have championed none of these species, favouring instead the dolphin.

In the 19th century, scientists began dissecting dolphin brains, and comparing brain capacity with body size, they concluded that the dolphin has the largest brain in proportion to its body size of any animal, including humans. Surely, some researchers thought, this must indicate great intelligence, perhaps superior to that of humans. It was an intriguing thought. A complete lack of understanding of dolphin behaviour coupled with the apparent charm of these animals with their perpetually smiling faces probably encouraged people to believe in their superhuman abilities. It must have been, and perhaps still is, easy to interpret dolphin behaviour by relating it to human behaviour. But what makes a good story does not necessarily make for good science.

Anatomically the dolphin brain is large and the neocortex – the part of the brain with which we create, innovate and reason – covers about 98 per cent of the surface. This compares with 96 per cent in humans and 69 per cent in kangaroos. It seems impressive, until we discover that the dolphin's neocortex is considerably thinner and less complex than the human brain's. During evolution, the dolphin brain became larger but not more complex. Comparable land mammals, such as humans, show much greater changes.

The human neocortex consists of densely packed columns of nerve cells, which are the processing units, interlaced with a complex microcircuitry; the areas of the brain associated with sensory systems are sandwiched within it. It is this integrated system that facilitates

DOLPHINESE Spectrograms show the clicks and echoes of a bottle-nosed dolphin examining fishing nets in Scotland's Firth of Forth.

memory and emotion and is critical for learning. The dolphin's neocortex, by contrast, has fewer but larger columns of nerve cells linked by less complicated wiring. It probably evolved to something like its present state more than 10 million years ago.

The environment in which the brain has evolved is also an important consideration. Humans developed dexterity and complex tool-use, walked upright, lived socially, invented a complex language, fostered the ability to think, and generally changed their environment to suit themselves. To achieve all this an animal would need a substantial neocortex.

The dolphin lives in the sea and has other demands on its brain. All mammals' brains carry out cognitive (information-gathering) functions and motor functions – sending instructions to the muscles and so on. But the dolphin's brain must also be continually monitoring what is up and what is down, how far away the surface is, when the air supply is going to run out, how far and how fast it can travel in one breath, what the surface conditions are like in order to take a breath without being swamped. The brain must carry out a series of complex calculations in order to make best use of each lungful of air. The dolphin is a social animal, too, and has developed

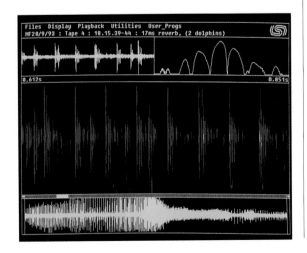

WHAT THE TRAINER SAYS *A dolphin carries out instructions from a blindfolded researcher.*

its own system of vocal communication which it uses not only to talk to its neighbours but also to find its way. A dolphin's life is dominated by sound.

Scientists have even speculated that the dolphin's sonar beam can scan the body of a fellow dolphin and evaluate its emotional state. Sound reflections from the beating heart, for example, may tell one dolphin whether the other is relaxed, tense or excited. With such a sophisticated sound system it is inevitable that the dolphin should have a brain able to process and act upon the sound information it produces and receives. Its large brain is not necessarily an indication of an advanced intelligence.

A large neocortex devoted to the processing of sound might indicate that the dolphin's echolocation system, like the human visual system, is its 'reality'. A sound picture represents its perception

HUNT THE TARGET *A dolphin touches the plastic tube holding a target. It had first examined the tube using echolocation.*

not only of the outside world, but also of self. And if dolphins are able to intercept each other's echoes, as bats can, then perhaps they have developed a communal sense of self – a group consciousness.

DO YOU SPEAK DOLPHIN?

There are those who believe that dolphins and their relatives have a sophisticated language of their own, which has become known as 'dolphinese'.

In an experiment in 1965, the US researcher Jarvis Bastion placed a pair of bottle-nosed dolphins in adjacent pools so that they were isolated visually yet could still hear each other. The female was taught to push paddles in order to receive a reward. The male had a similar set of paddles but received no training. Nevertheless he pushed the correct paddles and also obtained rewards. But it remains debatable whether he discovered the secret for himself by trial and error or had been told by his mate what to do. The results of the experiment are inconclusive, although

experience from the wild casts doubt on any sophisticated communication taking place. If dolphins can talk to each other it becomes hard to explain why so many ocean-going dolphins are killed in tuna purse-seine nets and why schools of pilot whales find themselves driven ashore and slaughtered on beaches in the Faeroes.

It is more probable that the dolphins' repertoire of whistles and burps are sound signatures needed for social grouping. The sender may simply be telling the rest of the group that he is present, although there is also some evidence to suggest that the way in which the call is given may indicate the individual's emotional state. Researchers have observed, for example, that the pitch and duration of the calls of captive dolphins change in stressful situations, such as being removed for veterinary examination.

SIGN LANGUAGE FOR DOLPHINS

A research facility in Hawaii has been focusing on this kind of research since the 1970s. Here, veteran dolphin researcher Louis Herman and his colleagues have been teaching bottle-nosed dolphins to respond to visual and sound signals.

The background to the research includes many years of study of the dolphin's sensory systems, particularly its capacity to see and hear, and its learning and memory capability. The dolphin has an excellent auditory memory, and is able to learn and remember long lists of sounds.

Herman wanted to know if language could be added to the dolphin's growing list of abilities. Instead of looking at the way a language might be produced, he concentrated on how an animal might understand language. To do this he copied the techniques used by second-language teachers who instruct pupils by getting them to carry out tasks. The level of understanding can be measured by how well the task is carried out.

Unlike sign-language experiments in which chimpanzees are invited to converse with words that might be open to misinterpretation, Herman started out simply to examine the cognitive characteristics of dolphins. He asked the questions: In what

do dolphins specialise? What are their limitations? And what role does intellect play in their lives?

At first one dolphin, a male called Ake, was taught a vocabulary in which human handlers used arm gestures and another, a female known as Phoenix, learned a set of acoustic sounds. Each gesture or sound represented objects and actions, such as 'Frisbee' or 'hoop'. The dolphins were asked to touch the objects; if they were correct, they received a 'yes' signal and a reward. If they got it wrong, they saw or heard a 'no' signal and got no reward. The dolphins, however, were sensitive to 'no' and became frustrated. They would aim a Frisbee or any other available object very accurately at the trainer, and so the 'no' signal was withdrawn. If they made an incorrect choice, the trainer simply turned his or her back.

After seven months' training the dolphins had a 20-word vocabulary and were

introduced to simple word combinations to see if they could take account of word order and syntax. Each dolphin learned a different system. The order of the acoustic signals given to Phoenix followed a more English style of sentence construction – subject, verb, object. The dolphin responded to commands such as 'Frisbee-fetch-basket', meaning, 'Collect the Frisbee and take it to the basket'. The arm signals given to Ake were presented in a more Germanic way with the verb at the end of the sentence. The same arm signal would be something like 'basket-Frisbee-fetch'.

The introduction of 'up', 'down', 'top', 'bottom' and 'gate' made the commands more complicated. 'Phoenix-Frisbee-fetch-gate', for example, meant that the female was asked to fetch the Frisbee and place it between two posts that served as a gate. There were also 'right' and 'left' signals and 'through', as in 'through-hoop'.

ALEX — THE PARROT WITH FEELINGS

The normally conservative scientific community was dumbfounded by Alex, the latest in a long line of seemingly intelligent animals. For Alex is not a chimpanzee or a dolphin, a sheepdog or a pet cat: Alex is an African grey parrot. He belongs to the American researcher Irene Pepperberg at the Northwestern University, Illinois, and since the late 1970s he has become a scientific celebrity.

There is nothing surprising in a parrot that can learn and mimic words. And Alex can, indeed, imitate the sounds of more than 80 English words. The remarkable thing about Alex is that he not only associates these words with objects or the qualities they describe, but also links two or more words together to convey new meaning.

Before Alex, a parrot was not

thought to be able to distinguish between, say, colours and shapes. Yet Alex has learned to distinguish between a blue key and a green ball or a green pen and a blade of grass, and what is more he says so. Alex can associate adjectives with nouns, and he can also appreciate quantity – up to six of anything – as well as quality. He also understands the concept of 'none'. In other words, he can appreciate the absence of something. If presented with two yellow pencils and asked 'How different?' he replies 'None'. But to the question 'How many?' he answers 'Two.'

Parrots in the wild are social animals and it is to be expected that a parrot, like any other social animal, would have an interest in communication. Alex is simply carrying on his ancestral tradition – except that in captivity he has been deprived of his native grey-

parrot 'language'. So he has learned to use whatever is available.

He has taken it a stage further. He has learned to do more than describe objects put before him; he can also express his wants and desires in what scientists describe as 'contextually appropriate vocalisation'. When Alex demands attention, he squawks, 'Come here,' and when bored with staying on his perch, he cries: 'Wanna go chair.' Professor Pepperberg has drawn parallels between Alex and a $2\frac{1}{2}$-year-old child. And, like a human infant who does not want to cooperate or is bored, Alex has discovered the power of the word 'No!'

THE ART OF CONVERSATION
Alex the African grey parrot achieves more than simple mimicry in his sophisticated conversations with people.

The dolphins were star pupils – responding equally well to both German and English-style instructions. They not only associated their visual or acoustic signals with actions or objects but also seemed to appreciate grammar. They successfully completed tasks after receiving commands made of sentences they had not encountered before, and even understood what to do when confronted with sentences constructed with different grammatical rules. When presented with complicated sentences, such as 'Frisbee-fetch-bottom-hoop' – which means 'Take the Frisbee to the hoop at the bottom of the tank' – Phoenix responded correctly, even when presented with it the first time. In doing so she ignored a ball floating on the surface and a hoop at the top of the tank.

They were sometimes asked to look for an object – a ball, say – that was not present. After a slight delay it was then put back in the tank along with an assortment of other items. The dolphin went straight for the correct object, showing that it understood the characteristic attributes the object possessed. It could also indicate that something was present or not by pressing 'yes' or 'no' paddles. Communicating in this way about an object that is not there indicates an appreciation of symbolism. The dolphin must have had a mental image of the missing object to have 'talked' about it.

Their exam results were very good; they performed tasks correctly about 85 per cent of the time. And they always understood the general sense of the word combination, even if they were not 100 per cent accurate in the interpretation. What the dolphins were demonstrating was that they understood both the meanings of words and how word order affects meaning. This, according to some philosophers and linguists, is central to human language and a sign of intelligence.

WHITHER INTELLIGENCE?

It is clearly very difficult not only to give a precise definition of intelligence but also to establish who or what is intelligent, whether a nonhuman animal or a human. Dolphins and primates, such as chimpanzees, gorillas, orang-utans, capuchin monkeys, vervets and baboons, seem more intelligent than most other animals, but there may be many forms of intelligence. A pigeon, for example, cannot find food in a maze as quickly as a rat can; on the other hand, it can find its way over distances of hundreds or even thousands of miles.

In truth, every species – from the amoeba to the blue whale – appears to have both an innate and a learned component in its behaviour. One definition of intelligence would be to consider as more intelligent those species in which the innate ingredient is lesser, and its capacity for learning far greater.

It was once thought that logical thought was unique to man, but it is hard to continue to believe this when we observe that monkeys in Africa or hummingbirds in North America are able to predict the time of year when they must go to very precise parts of their environment to find their preferred fruit or flowers. The more we study and observe, the more is revealed. Take nonhuman primates, for example.

The behaviour of monkeys – for instance, vervet monkeys and baboons – is

LANGUAGE OF BABOONS
Hamadryas baboons from Ethiopia have a complex communication system of sounds, gestures and body language.

A VOICE OF HIS OWN *The young proboscis monkey of South-east Asia has his own distinctive voice, recognised by others of his kind.*

much more complex than naturalists used to think, particularly when they communicate by sound and gesture and in social interactions. Like humans, monkeys hatch plots to seize power. One thing that distinguishes them from us is our articulated language; but is this sufficient to affirm that our intelligence is greater than theirs?

Vervet monkeys have specific alarm calls for particular predators and different grunts to address dominant or subordinate companions. The calls are not just automatic responses to fear or happiness, they mean something in the outside world. The alarm calls indicate where to run or look. When a juvenile vervet cries in distress, the other females in the troop will look directly at its mother. They can also recognise individuals by their voices. Monkey vocalisation is far more than a simple, involuntary expression of emotion. But here the story ends, for monkeys have their limitations.

Scientists believe that monkeys can 'read' one another's behaviour but cannot read each other's minds. Although they recognise individuals, they do not appreciate that others of their kind may possess knowledge that is different from their own. Also, many monkeys live in social groups in which none of their activities are private. They have little novel information to speak about, no secrets to share, no intimacies to withhold. In short, 'monkeys do not know what they know'.

Humanity's closest living relative, the chimpanzee, is much nearer to having what has been called a 'theory of mind' – that is, it is closer to attributing mental states to other individuals. Chimpanzees help each other, as in hunting. They share food, inform and deliberately misinform one another, come to the aid of their relatives, and set out to teach their youngsters – how to open a palm nut, for example. They recognise that thoughts bring about actions and their behaviour is calculated to influence the state of mind of other individuals. But even apes have problems in attributing specific mental states to others.

THE CHIMP WHO DIED OF GRIEF

There is the story, told by the British chimpanzee watcher Jane Goodall, of a young male chimpanzee whose mother had died. He avoided contact with other members of the group, stopped eating, spent hours in a hunched position, and rocked forlornly back and forth, looking to all the world like a human showing grief. After a few days he died. The young male had experienced a great sense of loss, but the other members of the group ignored him. Although the chimpanzee is able to grieve for a loved one, it is incapable of recognising the sense of loss in others and showing any empathy towards them. There is a limit, it seems, even to a chimpanzee's awareness of its world.

There are many similarities between our two species. There is a long period in which our children are dependent on their parents. The postures and gestures of our body languages are similar. Both live in what might be termed 'fission-fusion' groupings with individuals leaving the stable group (the family) to join another. In both species, there are expressions of emotion, signs of teaching and learning and a cultural tradition.

But there are attributes that even the wily chimpanzee cannot match. Humans have a complex symbolic language. Unlike the chimpanzee, we are able not only to show our offspring how to do something, but also to tell them how to do it and explain why it works that way. We have writing, records and history and can discuss events that happened in the near and distant past. We plan ahead, drawing up strategies and contingencies for the short-term and long-term future. We have abstract thoughts, mathematics, arts, sports, sciences, religions and philosophies. We can radically change our environment and influence the course of evolution.

Nevertheless, the scientific community is coming to believe that intelligence and awareness among nonhuman animals is a matter not of its presence or absence but of degree, kinds, richness and repertoire. Awareness and mental experiences are not denied to even the simplest of animals but there is a marked gradation throughout the animal kingdom, with an overwhelming gap between our closest ape relatives and ourselves. The question being asked today is less likely to be 'Which animals have mental experience and which do not?' and more likely to be 'Which animals have more, and how much more?'

HEARTBREAK *A wild chimpanzee grieves after his mother's death. He died soon after – not from disease but from a broken heart.*

INDEX

The editors are grateful to the following individuals and publishers for their kind permission to use material from the books below:

André Deutsch from The Education of Koko by Francine Patterson and Eugene Linden 1982.

Scientific American Inc. from Teaching Language to an Ape by Ann James Premack and David Premack 1972.